LIVING LIFE TO THE FULLEST

LIVING LIFE TO THE FULLEST

Disability, Youth and Voice

BY

KIRSTY LIDDIARD

University of Sheffield, UK

SALLY WHITNEY-MITCHELL

University of Sheffield, UK

KATY EVANS

University of Sheffield, UK

LUCY WATTS MBE

University of Sheffield, UK

RUTH SPURR

University of Sheffield, UK

EMMA VOGELMANN

University of Sheffield, UK

KATHERINE RUNSWICK-COLE

University of Sheffield, UK

AND

DAN GOODLEY

University of Sheffield, UK

United Kingdom – North America – Japan – India
Malaysia – China

Emerald Publishing Limited
Howard House, Wagon Lane, Bingley BD16 1WA, UK

First edition 2022

Reprints and permissions service
Contact: permissions@emeraldinsight.com

British Library Cataloguing in Publication Data
A catalogue record for this book is available from the British Library

ISBN: 978-1-83909-445-3 (Print)
ISBN: 978-1-83909-444-6 (Online)
ISBN: 978-1-83909-446-0 (Epub)

Printed and bound by CPI Group (UK) Ltd, Croydon, CR0 4YY

ISOQAR certified Management System, awarded to Emerald for adherence to Environmental standard ISO 14001:2004.

ISOQAR
REGISTERED

Certificate Number 1985
ISO 14001

INVESTOR IN PEOPLE

CONTENTS

List of Illustrations   *vii*

About the Authors   *ix*

Acknowledgements   *xi*

1. Living Life to the Fullest: Our Project   1
    Sally Whitney-Mitchell and Katy Evans

2. Theorising Disability: Towards a DisHuman Perspective   11
    Dan Goodley, Katherine Runswick-Cole and Kirsty Liddiard

3. Co-production, Participatory and Emancipatory Disability Research   25
    Kirsty Liddiard and Lucy Watts MBE

4. Posthuman Connections: Rethinking Animal–Human Relationships   43
    Katy Evans, Sally Whitney-Mitchell and Ruth Spurr

5. Disability and Faith   61
    Sally Whitney-Mitchell and Katherine Runswick-Cole

6. Rethinking Sexuality, Our Intimate Selves and Our Relationships
    with Others   79
    Katy Evans, Sally Whitney-Mitchell and Kirsty Liddiard

7. Labour in the Lives of Disabled Young People   99
    Katy Evans, Sally Whitney-Mitchell and Katherine Runswick-Cole

8. Making Meaningful Impact in and with Schools   115
    Greenacre Co-Researchers: Jemma, Marconi, Logan, Alex,
    Stevie and Emily; Harry Gordon and Kirsty Liddiard

9. Desiring Life and Living with Death   125
    Katy Evans, Sally Whitney-Mitchell and Kirsty Liddiard

References   *147*

Index   *165*

LIST OF ILLUSTRATIONS

Illustration 1: Image Description: Designed by Harry Gordon,
SEND Teacher, Greenacre School, This Diagram Shows
Our Methods of How We Explored the Notion of
Developing Questions for an Interview Schedule.   118

Illustration 2: Image Description: Harry Designed an Ethics Assault
Course, Set Out in the School Hall, Through Which
Greenacre Co-researchers Could Play with and Learn
About Ethical Considerations in Research. All of the
Activities Were Made Accessible for All Children,
Regardless of Disability, Impairment and/or Label.   119

ABOUT THE AUTHORS

Kirsty Liddiard is currently a Senior Research Fellow in the School of Education at the University of Sheffield and a theme Co-leader in iHuman. She is the author of *The Intimate Lives of Disabled People* (2018, Routledge) and the Co-editor of *The Palgrave Handbook of Disabled Children's Childhood Studies* (2018, Palgrave) with Tillie Curran and Katherine Runswick-Cole. She is also Co-editor of *Being Human in Covid-19* (in press, Bristol University Press) with Warren Pearce, Paul Martin and Stevie de Saille.

Sally Whitney-Mitchell is an Academic Researcher with a specialist interest in the lives of disabled young people, their access to work and the impact of assistance dogs in their lives. Using methods of co-production and virtual technologies, she works and writes (both academically and for wider audiences) from the comfort of her home as a co-researcher in various projects with the University of Sheffield, Scope, Youth Employment UK, Canine Partners and the Open University. She has consequently led the Canine Care Project in collaboration with Canine Partners, who partnered her with her own assistance dog Ethan. Both Ethan, and her strong faith, have helped her navigate her chronic, complex illnesses and spur her passion to make the most of every situation.

Katy Evans works as an Associate for Changing Our Lives, a rights-based organisation which champions the rights of disabled people and people with mental health difficulties to live ordinary lives. She was also an Advisor to the government during the 2014 Special Educational Needs and Disability reforms. Alongside this, she worked with the Council for Disabled Children to improve co-production with disabled young people nationally. She writes about her lived experiences of disability and being a trauma survivor and her difficulty accessing appropriate, non-pathologising mental health services. She has been a Co-researcher on the Living Life to the Fullest Project for four years and is keen to continue research in this field.

Lucy Watts MBE is a proud young disabled woman with a passion for the great outdoors, for writing and photography, who dedicates her time to making a difference for others and lives life to the fullest with support from her assistance dog Molly.

Ruth Spurr is a blogger and part-time model for Zebedee. She blogs about illness, youth, young people's lives and her assistance dog, Willow. Our Living Life to the Fullest Co-production Toolkit, *Why Can't We Dream?* was titled by her. She also regularly gives talks to primary school children on disability, her story and her mission to live life to the full.

Emma Vogelmann is a leading activist in the disabled community. She currently works as Lead Policy Adviser at Scope, on the children and young people team where she focusses on the issues faced by disabled children, young people and their families. Her main areas of focus are youth employment and inclusivity of disabled children.

Katherine Runswick-Cole is Professor of Education and Director of Research in The School of Education at the University of Sheffield, UK. She is known for her work critical disability studies and disabled children's childhood studies and is Co-editor of *The Palgrave Handbook of Disabled Children's Childhood Studies* (2018, Palgrave).

Dan Goodley is Professor of Disability Studies and Education and Co-director of iHuman, University of Sheffield. His recent publications include *Disability and Other Human Questions* (2020, Emerald) and *Disability Studies: An Interdisciplinary Introduction* (2016, Sage, Second Edition).

Harry Gordon is a UPS Teacher at Greenacre Special School in Barnsley. He has developed the research partnership between Greenacre School and the University of Sheffield's iHuman Research Institute. Through his passion for developing the ways in which schools and academies co-produce research in the classroom, he has championed a change in practice to enable Special Educational Needs and Disability students to have greater influence over the decisions that affect their lives. He and his students collaborated with Dr Kirsty Liddiard to co-produce the 'Why Can't We Dream?' toolkit (see Chapter 8). He is proud to lead Wellspring academy trust-wide training on co-producing research in the classroom: training practitioners in the methods, language and skills to enable young people with disabilities to have their voices heard on the issues that matter most to them.

ACKNOWLEDGEMENTS

Firstly, we would like to thank all of the children and young people and their families and allies who made The Living Life to the Fullest Project possible. The stories, contributions and energy you have shared with us are documented and honoured through this book.

This work was generously supported by the Economic and Social Research Council (ESRC) under grant ES/P001041/1, *Life, Death, Disability and the Human: Living Life to the Fullest*.

We also thank iHuman and the School of Education at the University of Sheffield for the continued support.

We thank our Community Research Partners, Impact Partners and other valued contributors for their support and insight throughout the project:

Purple Patch Arts
Pathfinders Neuromuscular Alliance
Good Things Foundation
Together for Short Lives
MDUK Trailblazers
Action Duchenne
Canine Partners
Louise Atkinson
Harry Gordon
Greenacre School, Barnsley and the Wellspring Academy Trust
Greenacre Co-researchers: Jemma, Marconi, Logan, Alex, Stevie and Emily
Rainbows Children's Hospice
Attenborough Arts Centre
Sipho Ndopu

We thank Carrie Aimes, an original member of The Co-Researcher Collective, who supported our early arts focus.

We would like to thank our assistance dogs, who have supported us in our work: Ethan, Folly, Willow and Molly.

We also thank Holly Yuille for her patient and kind contributions and expert proof-reading of the final drafts of many chapters in this book.

1

LIVING LIFE TO THE FULLEST: OUR PROJECT

SALLY WHITNEY-MITCHELL AND KATY EVANS

ACCESSIBLE SUMMARY

- This chapter introduces The Living Life to the Fullest Project: our research into the lives of disabled young people.

- We introduce The Co-Researcher Collective – a group of disabled young women who co-led the project.

- We tell you more about what follows in this book.

This book contains a multiplicity of voices: the voices of disabled young people, university academics and researchers and school children (specifically Chapter 8), all of whom have co-authored and contributed across chapters in order to make space for and document the human value of disability. Some of us write as disabled people. All of us write with personal experiences of disability in our families. As such, these voices have been central to the co-produced research project which sits at the very centre of this book: *Living Life to the Fullest: Life, Death, Disability and the Human* (ES/P001041/1; hereby The Living Life to the Fullest Project). Our project was funded by the Economic and Social Science Research Council and took place between 2017 and 2020. We tentatively began writing this book together in late 2019. Surely enough, as the Covid-19 global pandemic hit in spring 2020, and as a diverse research team working together, we began to realise this book's newfound importance and timeliness. Disabled people and their families became some of the hardest hit through the pandemic. Since March 2020, over 127,000 British people have lost their lives to Covid-19; and two-thirds of these have been disabled and chronically ill people, with people of colour and people with learning disabilities being disproportionately affected (Brothers, 2020). Thus, we began writing with gusto: eager to claim space to amplify the lives, hopes, desires and contributions of disabled children and young people living with life limiting and life-threatening impairments (LL/LTIs). We untangle such labels through each chapter as we come together as collaborators, co-authors and co-researchers. We want to clarify early here that this book is not a uniform research text. It is far more. This book represents to us a change to the standardised ways in which research is conducted, reported and written, typically only by academics and people in positions of power. Whilst this book *is* a coherent and reflexive account of our key findings across the project as they relate to the lives of disabled children and young people and their families, it is also a labour of love. It is a legacy. A legacy of our project, but also of the lives of The Living Life to the Fullest Project co-researchers, most of whom are living with LL/LTIs, and who are eager to leave their mark on the world. We hope, too, that is a readable and accessible text.

LIVING LIFE TO THE FULLEST

The Living Life to the Fullest Project was a three year co-produced arts-informed research project which aimed to explore the lives, hopes, desires and contributions of disabled children and young people living with LL/LTIs. Such impairments typically bring about short/er lives and life expectancies; it is a unique disability experience that has been both theoretically and empirically overlooked (see Runswick-Cole, 2010). It is important to say this early on that we used this kind of language – for example, 'life limiting' and 'life threatening' – within the project because it was familiar and known to our participants and their families. At the same time though, as disability researchers, disabled people and allies, we also resist these kinds of medicalising labels and understandings of disability; this is just one tension we explore through this book (see Chapter 2).

In The Living Life to the Fullest Project, we wanted to explore young people's lives in *full* and facilitate accessible ways for them to tell us about their own experiences. Co-researcher Emma, from The Co-Researcher Collective, highlighted that over her lifetime, although she had often been asked about her experiences, she felt many important topics were shied away from (Liddiard, 2018b, n.p.):

As a young disabled person I answer a lot of surveys on my
disability, my care and other similar topics. But I'm rarely asked
about what it is really like to be 24 and disabled. No one has asked
me whether I'm scared about my future or whether my life-limiting
condition has impacted my life choices. These are not pleasant
things to think about, but I can promise you, nearly every disabled
person has thought about them. When I was asked whether I
wanted to be a co-researcher for Living Life to the Fullest, I was
excited by the idea of a project that focuses on those unasked
questions. I wanted to help find out what our lives are really like
and how we really feel about them.

Emma's words encapsulate the driving force behind the project. The context of LL/LTIs tends to elicit feelings of pity and notions of despair (Runswick-Cole, 2010). However, for us this doesn't capture the richness of the lives of young people living with these types of impairments. Therefore, we wanted a project title that reflected this and challenged dominant notions of tragedy. Through the project, and this book, we highlight how disabled young people are living their lives to the fullest whilst not shying away from the many complexities involved doing so in a world shaped by ableist norms which routinely devalue them (Goodley, 2014). Ableism refers to a world view – a dominant reality – that assumes and values those deemed to be able-bodied and minded. In many ways, this research project and its findings became an act of resistance for both participants and co-researchers against ableism and also disablism. The latter refers to the specific forms of exclusion and marginalisation that people with sensory, physical and cognitive impairments are subjected to. So, our book makes mention of ableism and disablism: precisely because they often feature in the lives of people with LL/LTIs. If disability is but one element of the human condition; disability also poses a question – to what extent are disabled people allowed, supported and encouraged to live lives as human beings when they are so marked by disablism and ableism (Goodley, 2020)? Many Living Life to the Fullest Project co-researchers experienced this project as life changing as it provided a safe space to challenge their own internalised ableism and disablism (Reeve, 2002) and grapple with difficult concepts which often get silenced in the lives of disabled people. Possibly one of the ways we were able to elicit such rich, detailed accounts from our young participants was because we ourselves are disabled young people with similar experiences. We had the freedom to develop questions that perhaps other researchers had never dared to ask us. We recognised through this omission our experiences were going unheard and we wanted to put this right.

BACKGROUND TO THE PROJECT

As a project that sought to forge new understandings of the lives and contributions of disabled children and young people with LL/LTIs, The Living Life to the Fullest Project embodied the ethical and political principles of disabled children's childhood studies (Curran and Runswick-Cole, 2013, 2014; Runswick-Cole et al., 2018). This interdisciplinary field of research, writing and the arts actively positions the voices and experiences of disabled children and young people at the centre of inquiry. Or as Pluquailec (2018) suggests, as an approach to research it rightfully makes space to acknowledge disability as (positively) disruptive towards the typically ableist and disablist boundaries of research theory and practice (see Chapter 3). In the context of our project, we understood co-production as an aspirational approach where academics work together with a range of partners to produce research and outcomes not possible in isolation (Runswick-Cole et al., 2017). According to Durose et al. (2012, p. 2), co-produced research 'aims to put principles of empowerment into practice, working "with" communities and offering communities greater control over the research process'. For Olsen and Carter (2016, p. 7), the co-production of knowledge 'can promote respectful integration of ideas'. By extension, then, for us research is not a process about or for disabled children and young people with LL/LTIs and their families, but conducted with and by them (see Fudge et al., 2007). Moreover, the research questions, methods, strategies of analysis and plans for impact and public engagement reflect the ambitions of disabled children and young people and their families and community stakeholders. Thus, co-production became a necessary part of shaping inquiry at the very early stages, prior even to any funding.

As such, our bid for funding was co-authored in collaboration with disabled children and young people, their parents, carers and allies and key representative non-governmental organisations (NGOs) Purple Patch Arts, The Good Things Foundation and Pathfinders Neuromuscular Alliance, who later became our funded research partners. In this context, co-writing for us involved the discussion of ideas and research and impact planning through a number of writing workshops and meetings. We asked disabled children and young people many questions, such as: What should we be asking questions about in the research? Who should we be asking? What aspects of your life often go unnoticed that you would like to see explored in this project? What would enable you to participate in our research if you wanted to? How can we make it easier/appealing for you and other disabled young people to take part? What do we need to get right in our project? What could we get wrong? With permission, we posed these questions via a short accessible film posted to the Facebook pages of disabled young people's organisations and related charities. Disabled young people either 'commented' below our posts or sent an email containing their thoughts.

Ultimately, our emphasis at this early time was to work in ways that ensured the inception of the research process was both accessible and enacted a shared distribution of responsibility from the outset. Integral to this was our Research Management Team – at that time made up of disabled and non-disabled academics (at a variety of career levels, from PhD to Professor); young people with LL/LTIs; parents and family members; allies and campaigners; researchers, practitioners and representatives of our NGO and community research and impact partners, many of whom occupy several of these subject positions. They invited us to engage with their communities outside of the academic context. The Co-Researcher Collective – established later in the project (after funding had been awarded) – quickly overtook Research Management Team as the day-to-day leadership of the project. Ultimately, we critically engaged with a co-production methodology that provided space for partners to inform the running of the project, the kinds of findings that emerge and ideas for impact and public engagement that were creative rather than prescriptive. Co-production can be a contested field, but we purposefully made space for unknowing and uncertainty, letting research relationships with disabled young people and partner organisations lead, with the aim that stakeholders take ownership of the research in ways unforeseeable at that time.

The Co-Researcher Collective consists of six disabled young people (all women) who live with LL/LTIs. In recruiting co-researchers, the only 'criteria' placed upon participation was a desire to explore disabled young people's lives and contribute to the process through undertaking project-related activities of co-researchers' choice. Initial groundwork to build the Collective began early in the process – after funding was awarded and following co-authoring the bid for funding. After meeting Lucy Watts MBE, a prolific young disabled campaigner who currently serves as an Ambassador for the national charity Together for Short Lives – and now Lead Co-researcher in The Living Life to the Fullest Project – we were advised as to the benefits of online spaces towards building meaningful relationships with disabled young people. Lucy explained how virtual environments are critical to her advocacy and activist work and, in short, we listened, and this conversation significantly shaped inquiry moving forward. From this, online advertising through the project website and social media led to prospective co-researchers making initial contact (typically through Facebook Messenger) and eventually joining the Collective, enabling a radical revision of the didactic ways in which research into disabled young people's lives is typically carried out.

THE CO-RESEARCHER COLLECTIVE: NEW WAYS OF WORKING

The entire project, including the writing of this book, involved us all working together as a Collective and adopting new ways of working. As mentioned above, the project was co-led by disabled young people via The Co-Researcher Collective and three university-based academics, each who themselves have lived experience of disability in different ways – as disabled people, carers and allies. We sought to use anti-ableist and anti-disablist approaches that often involved being creative in how we approached research tasks. This included using virtual spaces and methods for research; creating an environment in which we could be open about and identify each other's differences and needs; understanding the importance of taking our time, and incorporating this understanding into our working practices (see Chapters 3 and 7). The creativity elicited from these ways of working as a Collective highlighted the possibilities of what disability can bring to everyday life, as well as research practices and inquiry. As a Collective, we understood the value of disability and difference and that, by their very nature, these unique ways of being can be positively disruptive to normative ways of working (see Chapter 7).

Initially The Co-Researcher Collective came together as a group of relative strangers but over the course of this project our relationships with one another have evolved into something none of us predicted. For us, as disabled young people exploring the life experiences of our peers, it was inevitable that we were going to be personally touched by the data and broader material. For many of us it was the first time we saw our own experiences reflected back at us and our collaborative discussions enabled us to challenge our internalised ableism. One of the few times we met in a physical space was at the project's residential Analysis Retreat where we analysed our data together, immersing ourselves in participants' stories and sharing our own experiences as part of the analytical process (see Chapter 3). This was a very impactful time for those involved and we believe that being together in a safe space allowed a greater emotionality into the process as we examined our own lives. In fact, each one of us shed a tear during this time. We feel the mutual understanding and friendships that have developed through our meetings and WhatsApp conversations have led to increased intimacies, facilitating a richer content for this book. The Co-researcher Collective became a force of its own and our relationships became deeper than a team simply collecting and analysing data together. We have both commiserated and celebrated with each other through life events from moving locations and struggling to recruit personal assistants to finally being successful in winning 'fights' for funding. Throughout, there has been an innate understanding of the challenges these things pose and it has become a safe space to voice these frustrations within the group where so often these experiences are silenced. In many ways, we created a solidarity between us which Ahmed (2004, p. 189) notes:

> *Solidarity does not assume that our struggles are the same struggles, or that our pain is the same pain, or that our hope is for the same future. Solidarity involves commitment, and work, as well as the recognition that even if we do not have the same feelings, or the same lives, or the same bodies, we do live on common ground.*

Furthermore, the 'access intimacy' that Mia Mingus (2011) discusses in her blog about crip solidarity was at the heart of the project and strengthened the bonds within The Co-Researcher Collective and broader team. To clarify our use of the word crip, we follow Hamraie and Fritsch (2019, p. 2) and reify it as 'the non-compliant, anti-assimilationist position that disability is a desirable part of the world'. Mingus (2011, n.p.) explains:

> *[...] access intimacy is that elusive, hard to describe feeling when someone else 'gets' your access needs. The kind of eerie comfort that your disabled self feels with someone on a purely access level.*

This access intimacy that we enact together as a team denotes closeness, friendship and solidarity in our project as ways to extend thinking about the affective politics and emotionality of inquiry. We note this here, because despite these intimacies, in nearly four years of working closely together, we have seldom ever been in the same room, or shared physical space. Our point here, then, is to counter normative ideas of face-to-face work as a point of superiority in qualitative research and to affirm technologies as spaces ripe for human and affective connection, nurture and care, especially for marginalised people who experience barriers in the physical and social world.

Co-researcher Sally summarises [and writes] what crip solidarity has meant to her: Joining The Co-Researcher Collective has benefitted me personally in addition to being a group doing fab quality research into the lives of young, disabled people. This is because it is a group formed of amazing, strong, young disabled women who are making waves in and outside the spheres of disability studies and activism. They have challenged me to believe in myself more, value and trust my own experience and allowed me the space to grow in the field of research. Not only that but they are bold, powerful women who have taught me that I am far more capable than I realise and inspired me to push the limits of my own and society's expectations.

Everyone involved in The Living Life to the Fullest Project has been keen for its impact to reach beyond inquiry and the words you will read in this book. It is our wish that this inspires a shift in how research with disabled young people is conducted and truly embeds the principles of co-production, as opposed to the often tokenist efforts to include disabled young people in research (Whitney et al., 2019; Liddiard et al., 2018). In our project, disabled young co-researchers had the flexibility and influence to steer the direction of this project. Arguably, the final result is something which likely would not have had the chance to materialise had it been led only by academics based in universities. As a way to encourage this kind of co-production to take place within other settings and across projects we have developed a co-production toolkit that we titled *Why Can't We Dream?* as one of the key legacies of this project (https://whycantwedream.co.uk/). We discuss the toolkit and its application in Chapter 8.

WHAT FOLLOWS IN THIS BOOK?

Whilst we have tried to capture and portray the wide range of topics that disabled young people discussed in our research, a book such as this could not reflect the vastness and depth of issues raised. This book serves to highlight some of the key themes that emerged from our collaborative analysis that we have deemed pertinent to representing the realities of our disabled young participants living with LL/LTIs. However, every disabled young person experiences life differently and will always have different stories to tell. We hope this book introduces the reader to this rich and much needed area of study.

It was our intention all along to make this book as accessible as possible to ensure that a diverse range of people could take something from it, whether that be social workers, academics, students, young people or families. We were particularly keen for it to be accessible to disabled young people themselves. Although the life experiences and the paths that led us to working together as a Co-Researcher Collective were diverse, what united us was a sense of loneliness some of us had all experienced at various points in our lives as disabled young people. We therefore wanted the book to represent the solidarity of disabled young people in living their lives despite the challenges often involved in living within and through ableist contexts that often exclude us (see Chapter 2). It is our hope that disabled young people will feel reassured that they are not alone in their experiences, in the same ways we all did when we came together as a Collective. For many co-researchers, this book became a personal legacy, a way to leave a mark on the world and carry our messages forward when we are no longer here. We will talk more about the importance of our legacies in Chapter 9.

What follows in this book, then, is an elaboration of our project. In Chapter 2, we set out our theoretical underpinnings and perspectives, which routinely changed through the project as we co-built theory as a diverse team together. Chapter 3 explains our revolutionary methodology for carrying out authentically co-produced research which centred disabled young people in the research process as both participants and co-researchers. In Chapter 4, we use posthumanist theories of disability to look at the effects of relationships between disabled young people and assistance dogs. This chapter also highlights a small impact project that evolved from The Living Life to the Fullest Project, The Canine Care Project (Whitney et al., 2020). Chapter 5 explores the little-researched area of disability and faith and focusses on the experiences of one of the co-researchers and a few project participants who identified faith as very important in their lives. In Chapter 6, we lead a discussion around the intersections of disability, sexuality and relationships, based on disabled participants' reflections on their own intimate selves, lives and futures. In Chapter 7, we discuss the concept of work and the movement away from normative understandings of labour, with a particular focus on the emotional labour carried out by disabled young people. Chapter 8 explores working with children and young people in special educational need and disability educational contexts and the power of research and inquiry as a unique form of emancipatory pedagogy. Finally, we conclude this important co-authored book in Chapter 9, where we reflect on the outlook of disabled young people and the delicate balance of a desire to live life fully whilst holding the concept and reality of death and dying simultaneously.

2

THEORISING DISABILITY: TOWARDS A DISHUMAN PERSPECTIVE

DAN GOODLEY, KATHERINE RUNSWICK-COLE AND KIRSTY LIDDIARD

ACCESSIBLE SUMMARY

- In this chapter, we engage with theory, exploring different ways of thinking about the human.

- We look at disabled young people's lives in relation to theory.

- We talk about a theoretical 'model' we have called the DisHuman.

INTRODUCTION

This book is built upon an assumption that social theories can be generated through a meaningful engagement between the authors of this book: university-based researchers and a Co-Researcher Collective of disabled young people. Our text brings together a team of co-researchers as theoretical provocateurs and theorists in their own right who, through their activism and writing, are challenging us to reconsider the meaning of life, death and disability. Their work for The Living Life to the Fullest Project has enabled us as a team to consider the promise and potential of different theories and research methods. In this chapter, we focus on theory. We begin by outlining an approach – critical disability studies – the grounding and foundational interdisciplinary approach of our research. Within this brief introduction to this perspective we introduce a number of developments that give the reader a flavour of this approach. We are drawn to an important relationship that disability studies have enjoyed with humanism: a dominating philosophical perspective in Western and European countries. Humanism has served disabled people – especially in terms of human right discourses – though remains stubbornly exclusionary in terms of the kinds of humanities that are deemed valuable. We therefore move onto an overview of the critical posthumanities: an emerging philosophical community that we find to be more inclusive of disabled people not least through its emphasis on 'Missing People's humanities'. Finally, we reflect on the relative merits of humanist and posthuman approaches and, very much in line with a 'having your cake and eating it' approach to life, we propose a generative perspective that sits in between, across and through and with these two perspectives: one we define as a DisHuman perspective. We assert that as a research team we are engaging with a DisHuman approach to theory and activism: one that blends the pragmatics of humanism with post-human possibilities. By this we mean that many disabled young people desire to be recognised by the dominant philosophy that underpins moral, political and legal life (humanism). Yet, at the very same time, disability demands more collectivist and expansive models of human life (posthuman). A DisHuman position captures this complexity; offering a responsive theoretical perspec-tive to work in unison with the dynamic bodies and minds of those living with shorter lives.

CRITICAL DISABILITY STUDIES

This book is a contribution to the growing field of critical disability studies. Some of us have written elsewhere about this emergent field of scholarship and activism (Goodley, 2012, 2016; Runswick-Cole et al., 2018; Liddiard, 2018a). There are many debates associated with this growing field and we do not have the space nor the inclination to cover them all. Instead, we hand-pick a number of themes associated with the emergence of critical dis-ability studies that have influenced and been shaped by The Living Life to the Fullest Project. To be critical suggests some kind of revision, reframing and revisiting of the foundations of what has already become understood as disability studies (Goodley et al., 2019). And this is what critical disability studies does; it builds on an established field (disability studies) and reflects critically on the ways in which the field might be further enhanced to support and understand the lives of all disabled people; in our case young people with life-limiting and life-threatening impairments (LL/LTIs). The study of disability has traditionally been the remit of health and psychological sciences as they probed the disabling impacts of physical, sensory and cognitive impairments. These professions have created individual, psychological and medical models of disability; essentially approaches that understand disability in terms of individual deficit or lack and as a private trouble. In contrast, critical disability studies understands disability as a social, cultural, historical and political entity. Many people with impairments are disabled; in the sense that they are dehumanised, devalued and denigrated by societies that associate the presence of impairment with lack, failing and deficit. Disability studies turn the finger of blame away from individual impairment onto society. And this shift of attention – from disability-as-impairment to disability-as-social oppression – energised activists and academics came to promote social, political, cultural and historical models of disability. The late Mike Oliver, the first Professor of Disability Studies in Britain, was instrumental in developing the social model of disability as a conceptual tool for reframing disability as a social and political concern. His text – the *Politics of Disablement* – remains a classic in the field (Oliver, 1990). It clearly articulated the ways in which the lives of people with impairments are subject to the limitations of material barriers including inaccessible physical environments, exclusionary work practices and wholly inadequate legislation (e.g. Oliver, 1990). Critical disability studies research maintains this socio-cultural and historical understanding of disability. However, it builds upon this sociological imagination in a number of ways: not least in acknowledging that society and culture are perpetually changing and ever-morphing. To be critical is to constantly consider and reconsider whether or not theories of disability studies are up to the job of making sense of the contemporary moment. We understand critical disability studies as a coming-of-age: a realisation of over 30 years of theorising, research, policy and practice building on the work of founding figures like Oliver.

Critical disability studies acknowledge the importance of new developments in technology. All of us are touched by digital worlds. The pandemic has illuminated many aspects of our contemporary society; not least a reliance we all have upon our digital connections. While there are digital divides between disabled and non-disabled people – with the latter more likely to be able to access digital platforms and communities more than the former – our sense of identities, relationships and communities are being fundamentally reshaped by our experiences as digital humans (Goggin and Newell, 2003, 2007; Googin, 2018). Hence, any study of disability developed, say, in the 1990s will fail to be in tune with the realities of digital life in the 2020s (post-Covid-19). Critical disability studies are sensitive to the rapid developments in AI, Big Data, digitisation, robotics and automation (Ellis et al., 2018). Disability, like any social and cultural phenomenon, can be understood as an entity fabricated not only in physical environments but, increasingly, in digital worlds. Our daily engagements with social media and our usage of the many communication platforms become wrapped up in our identities, relationships and communities. This is not to say that we should become uncritical technophiles. While new technologies have enhanced the lives of disabled people we should be wary of technology driving advances rather than the desires and needs of disabled people. Nevertheless, online platforms and digital culture hold great promise and potential for disabled people. And, as we shall explore later in the book, online research methodologies offer distinct possibilities for including disabled researchers in expansive and productive ways (see Chapter 3).

Critical disability studies also acknowledge the centrality of the perspectives and expertise of disabled young people themselves. Hitherto, disability studies have developed in ways that were disconnected from studies of childhood and youth. And yet, from the other side of the argument, studies of childhood and young people have been stubbornly resistant to the contributions of disability studies. Disabled children and young people have, for many years, occupied a liminal space: an inbetween no-man's land devoid of recognition, research and scholarship. The development of disabled children's childhood studies (Runswick-Cole et al., 2018) foregrounds the lives of disabled young people and does so in ways that have ripple effects upon childhood, youth and disability studies. One of these repercussions is the requirement to acknowledge that disabled young people are not simply objects of study and intervention (in the sense of ensuring that their lifeworlds are explicitly engaged with in research and policy making) but they are also active subjects and theorists of their own lives (so repositioning them as research experts). This analytical move is key to our research: not least in bringing together academic researchers and co-researchers where the latter group are constituted by theorists and researchers who also identify as disabled young people.

A further marking of research as critical disability studies is an acknowledgement of the complexities of theorising and theory making. Sophisticated theories will inevitably be developed as a consequence of trying to understand what it means to live as a disabled young person in advanced capitalist societies that are increasingly shaped by new technological developments. As Braidotti (2013) acknowledges, social theory is often notoriously slow at keeping in time with rapid developments of everyday social life. And this time-lag risks failing to represent the complex realities of the lives of disabled young people. It is therefore incumbent upon us to work diligently but also responsively with disabled young people to make sense of the here and now of disability while always being aware of the histories that under-gird phenomena that can easily be simplistically understood as ephemeral and transitory. It is easy, for example, to dismiss digital identities as (yet another) example of superficial and transitory phenomena associated with advanced capitalism. One might also want to ask how established concepts such as community are extended and reworked in digital spaces.

Critical disability studies has, understandably, kept a strong focus on disability and the lives of disabled people. However, this has been supplemented by a dual consideration of ability and the dominating influence of non-disabled people on the constitution of disability. In order for disability to be conceived it has to be done so in relation to its opposite; ability (Goodley, 2014). Hence, the concept of dis/ability permits us to consider the co-constitution of disability and ability. One cannot exist without the other. Disability comes to be known as the absence of ability and disabled people are valued (or often devalued) by a common-sensical view; that being able-bodied or able-minded is preferential to being physically, sensorially or cognitively disabled. For those readers of a philosophical persuasion, this recognition of the binary play of ability and disability is part of the poststructuralist movement of the 1960s and 1970s. Writers such as Derrida and Foucault pushed scholars and activists to consider the ways in which black-white, female-male, poor-rich and, later, disabled-abled are always made in relation to one another. In order to even contemplate the meaning of disability it is absolutely essential that we understand the ways in which ability is constructed through various social discourses. We need to recognise that being able equates with being a valued member of society. But that this, often, uncritical acceptance of ability – as if it were a natural part of the human condition – needs shaking up. We have witnessed the development of critical whiteness, masculinity, heteronormative and occidental studies often generated in response to the rich resources offered by black, feminist, queer and postcolonial fields of enquiry (see Goodley et al., 2019 for an overview). And, relatedly, critical disability studies has supported a burgeoning critical ableist studies and dis/ability studies that seek to understand but also contest the exclusionary impact of ableism: the tacit, deep-rooted and institutionally ingrained reification of autonomy, independence and self-sufficiency. Our text, then, is written in the shadow of ableism.

In response to the last point, critical disability studies herald a time of co-production. It is fair to say that disability studies has enjoyed a historical engagement with more inclusive modes of research production. Participatory, inclusive and action research models have enjoyed currency from the very time the study of disability shifted from individual failing to societal barriers (e.g. Barton and Oliver, 1997; Barton and Clough, 1998). Critical disability studies enjoys an engagement with new iterations of what has become known as co-production (see Nind, 2014; Strnadová et al., 2014, 2015). Co-production seeks to break with old hierarchies of researcher and researched and, in its place, posit a more democratic philosophy and reality of research production. The utopian scenario is a horizontal playing field where academics and non-academic university researchers work collaboratively together to research and change the world. The pragmatic reality of co-production might not always fit with this utopia. And, as we articulate in this book, the challenges of co-production are not to be diminished nor under-played. That said, co-production offers so much; not least in bringing in the unique perspectives of disabled young people who are theoreticians and analysts in their own right. This is a central message of this book and also critical disability studies: that the meanings attached to disability, life and death are up for grabs and not simply the prerogative of academics, practitioners nor policy makers.

Critical disability studies has also increasingly attended to the ways in which disability is not simply experienced, constituted nor materially created in the social world. Disability is also felt; that is to say it has an affective or emotional quality (Goodley et al., 2018c). Emotional and disabled lives converge in complex ways, and, crucially, affect and disability can only ever be understood in the context of a contemporary cultural moment that emphasises able-bodied-and-mindedness as the preferential experiential position from which to live a valued human life. Whenever we talk, then, of emotions associated with disability, it is crucial that we do not ignore the ideology of ableism that under-scores how we are expected to feel about our lives. Our text, then, is sensitive to the ways in which the 'good life' is conceptualised and felt in our emotional lives (Johnson and Walmsley, 2010). Too often a good life is defined in terms of a life well lived; a productive one that does not end too soon, associated with making a valued economic, educational and cultural contribution. And when one feels that we have not met these standards of human productivity this can be upsetting and unsettling. But this narrowed sense of valued humanness is inherently ableist: based upon a very humanist register (one we will explore below). These formations of the 'good life' already have an idealised human being in mind. The truth is that life is not so narrow, nor linear nor predictable. And, in this book, we want to reclaim our shared precarity as human beings. In order to understand how emotion and disability interact we can only do so by acknowledging the complexity of humanity. And part of this complexity is the human need for connection with others and the centrality of interdependence.

As Ahmed (2004, 2010) has beautifully articulated, our feelings are hugely influenced by the ways in which emotions circulate in and through different economies of affect. Love, for example, is highly regulated and influenced by marketing, consumption, popular culture and therapeutic discourses. While emotions are felt as internal psychological states they are always influenced by material, cultural and economic forces. The work of Thomas (2007) has been incredibly powerful in the field of critical disability studies in terms of unpicking the ways in which disabled people come to experience negative affective and emotional states that are the direct consequences of being belittled, dehumanised and oppressed. Hence, a lowered sense of self-esteem is often hugely influenced by a disabling society that devalues the very idea of being disabled. Just as external barriers create material obstacles (such as unemployment, inaccessible physical environments or educational exclusion) so internalised barriers risk creating psycho-emotional barriers (a sense that one is not welcome, adequate enough to work or to be educated). To this complex affect economy we would add ableism. This philosophy upholds unrealistic standards of economic achievement and psychological well-being. And a sense of failure is always felt emotionally. If we live in a disabling world that devalues disabled people – and we occupy a culture that inherently values able-bodied-and-mindedness – then it is entirely understandable that the subsequent emotional responses might be negative and harmful. These disablist and ableist affect economies require unpicking and contesting. And our text brings together a research team that seeks to engage in these dual processes of analysis and intervention.

HUMANISM

Our overview of critical disability studies has unpacked what we have identified as some of the themes and debates, within the literature, that we think resonate with the lives of disabled young people with LL/LTIs. We weaved in and out of some of the ways in which disability and ability are understood. We want to use this section to delve a little deeper into a dominant philosophy that undergirds contemporary cultures and societies: humanism. Our excavation of the philosophy of humanism begins with a well-worn story from disability studies; the prominence of the medical model in people's understandings of disability. From 'the medical model perspective', Shyman (2016, p. 368) writes 'the locus of the disability itself lies within the person, leaving the need for treatment to come from an external counteractive source'. It follows, then, he continues

that the focus of treatment from the medical model perspective
must be on either rehabilitating such difficulties that are caused by
the disability or curing the individual of that disabling condition in
order to attain, or approach, normality.

We have learnt from generations of disability studies scholars that the medical model powerfully shapes how we understand disability; typically in terms of tragedy, pathology and deficit. We need to be clear here. We are not writing against the life-giving work of medicine in our lives. Medicine is, for many disabled and non-disabled people, a matter of life or death. Medicine sustains and enhances lives. Our concern lies more with *medicalisation*: a persuasion that shoe-horns all perspectives into a grand narrative dominated by the vocabularies of medicine. Medicalisation refers to the institutionalisation of medical knowledge as *the* knowledge through which to make sense of human diversity and deviations from human norms. Rayner et al. (2010) detail the interlinking of pharmaceutical companies, private healthcare, medical authority and popular discourse that come together under different regimes of medicalisation to offer persuasive and expert accounts of human anomalies. The regimes are not simply offering practical ideas, theories or solutions; they are wrapped up with what Mike Oliver (1990) termed the restoration of normality. But this begs the question; how are we understanding normality? An answer lies in another dominating belief system in contemporary society; that of liberal humanism. St. Pierre (2015, pp. 331–332) offers us a really helpful overview and it's worth giving space to an extended quotation from their lovely writing:

Liberal humanism is a broad-based political and intellectual
emergence within the Enlightenment, which gained full ascendency
in the 19th and 20th centuries, valuing 'open and undogmatic
inquiry, freedom of the individual conscience' and aiming for a
'respect for social justice, social and psychological utility, decency,
[and] liberality' (Coates and White, 1970, p. 447). At its center,
liberal humanism is a marriage between the long humanist tradition
and liberal ideals: a dual commitment to 'man' and 'freedom'.
However, in its effort to secure 'man' as a completely autonomous
being, liberalhumanism must first transcend group differences and
generalize attributes of humanity in a movement of essentialization.

'The story of humanism', Scott (2000, p. 119) writes, 'is often told as a kind of European coming-of-age story'. This coming of age is associated with many things that denote human progress; mind over matter, the generation of liberal democracies, a secular celebration of science over religion, the emergence of human potency and the taming of wild nature. Humanism is the constitution of the human being as the epicentre of inquiry. Humanism is a philosophy born out of human progression. And to many people, even today, humanism is the desired philosophical constitution of the human as omnipotent. Now, what does this have to do with medicalisation of disabled people and the restoration of normality?

While curing or rehabilitating those recovering from illness appears in the world as a seemingly value-free desirable aspiration of medicine, medicalisation is a ramping up of these practices in the pursuit of a restoration of an idealised form of normality. Implicit within the practice of medicalisation is the restoration of normality; not a normality objectively framed through the discourses of science (if we are to accept that such a framing could take exist in the first place) but a normality framed in the image of humanism (and tied to it idealised formations of what it means to be human). This humanist normality, as St. Pierre (2015), is one associated with an articulate, healthy, willing and able citizen. And the willing, ready and able individual is precisely the kind of citizen required of our contemporary societies (Goodley, 2020). Liberal humanism incubates the production of a particular kind of cherished human. And like any cherished social category we human beings desire being included in this category.

Human rights discourses enshrine this category in legislative documents. The United Nations Convention on the Rights of Persons with Disabilities is but one example of a discourse that seeks to recognise the human rights of disabled people. And within this document is the humanist impulse to draw disabled people into the category of human. The fact that this discourse is required in the twenty-first century is a stark reminder that disabled people are all too often not considered to be as human as other human beings. When governments ratify this convention they are not just demonstrating a commitment to recognising disabled people as humans with rights. These governments are also indicating that their nation states have historically failed to assign these human qualities to disabled people. But this begs a question: why would anyone want to be recognised by a discourse (human rights) that has historically excluded them? A pragmatic response would emphasise the work done by the discourse; emphasising disabled people's rights to access education, work and their communities as equal members of the global human race. A philosophical response would be more critical; is there something exclusionary built into the very idea of human rights that, by definition and comprehension, has the potential to always exclude certain groups of people? And if this is the case then why would we want to keep hold of a humanist tradition that has always excluded some categories of human? These critical questions lead us into another philosophical approach: the critical posthumanities.

CRITICAL POSTHUMANITIES

We are deeply inspired by the work of the feminist philosopher Rosi Braidotti (2013, 2019). Her work has been incredibly important in helping to generate a new philosophical space; the critical posthumanities. This approach might be viewed as a reaction and collectivist response to the limits of humanism. If humanism is built on the notion of 'I think, therefore I am' the posthuman might be coined by the phrase 'I am interconnected, therefore we are'. As Braidotti (2019, p. 35) writes, 'the posthuman turn shows that the consensus about the universal value of Eurocentric assumptions about "Man" has dissipated and this figuration of the human is in trouble'. As we considered above humanism gives with one hand (enshrining an idealised version of autonomous humanness with all the associated trappings) and takes with the other (marginalising those human beings who fail to embody the necessary autonomy expected of these humanist citizens). Critical posthumanities has the potential to actualise the development of what Braidotti (2019, p. 51) terms of 'Missing People's Humanities'. We know that many human groups have been excluded from the humanist hegemony including black, queer, trans, female, migrant, refugee, first nations, indigenous and disabled people. Exclusion can breed resistance and it is clear that disabled people have throughout history found imaginative and sustainable ways of living that embrace support, care and interdependence. A posthuman philosophy responds well to these imaginative forms of interdependency because of its emphasis on the extended nature of humanity (Goodley et al., 2014b, 2018a). We have entered, she suggests, the epoch of 'panhumanity' where each and everything is technologically mediated. Human beings have never been more powerful (a state of affairs described as the Anthropocene), more technologically advanced (in the midst of a technologically driven 4th Industrial revolution) or more at risk (referenced as the 6th Extinction as evidenced by the impacts of global warming). This strange paradox of humankind – where our species is enhanced by science, augmented by technology but also threatened by the impacts of our destructive actions on the planet – remains a perennial problem for researchers across the arts, humanities, natural and social sciences. Human predicaments are also those of the planet and its inhabitants. There is an urgent need to find more effective interconnections to address these predicaments. The challenges human beings face are deeply entangled in their relations with non-human animals, other humans, machines and their environments. These entanglements are ever-changing, fluid and shifting dynamics. Often, the scholarly and popular framings of these dynamics are wholly negative; climate change, species extinction, genetic modification, synthetic farming, the widespread adoption of drones, the AI and robotic take-over, ubiquitous digitalisation and Big Data. We flirt with dystopia; pitching humans, animals, machines and environments against one another. Such a view fuels apocalyptic moral panics, breeds paranoia and entrenches artificial distinctions between humans and non-humans. In contrast, recent scholarship from within the social sciences, arts and humanities has made a strong case for thinking more positively, affirmatively and creatively about human beings' shared obligations to machines, animals and environments (as well as with other humans) (see Chapter 4). What generative hopes and opportunities can be found in these established and new interrelations? Let us tease out three key elements of this approach borrowing from Braidotti's (2013) *The Posthuman* and Goodley et al.'s (2014b) *Posthuman Disability Studies.*

Life beyond the body: We live in times of human enhancement, gene therapy, artificial intelligence, automation and digital culture. These scientific developments have had a huge impact on the human body. For Braidotti (2013, p. 35), biological matter is no longer dialectically opposed to culture, nor to technological mediation, but continuous with both of these modes. Contemporary science and biotechnologies affect the very fibre and structure of the living and have 'altered dramatically our understanding of what counts as the basic frame of reference for the human today' (Braidotti, 2013, p. 40). The biological has morphed into the biotechnical, biocultural and biodigital. Our bodies are increasingly extended, distributed and interconnected with our offline and online environments.

Life beyond the human species: A posthuman philosophy emphasises our interconnections with other non-human animals. Braidotti (2013, p. 668) writes, drawing on the work of Borges, we think of animals in terms of a taxonomy of three groups: those we eat, those we watch TV with and those we are scared of. We confine animals into a host of instrumental, oedipal or phantasmagorical relationships. But how might we think again about our alliances with animals? One answer, clearly, is through our interconnections and vitality of bonds associated with us sharing a planet. This vital interconnection posits a qualitative shift of relationship away from species-ism and towards an ethical appreciation of what bodies (human, animal, others) can do. Animals are not simply objects of attachment, assistance nor affection: human–animal interrelations offer key opportunities for approaching methods that sustain human and non-human species. As the pandemic has brutally demonstrated; human and animal species are interlinked and interconnected (see Chapter 4).

Life beyond death: A humanist philosophy emphasises human beings. Such a bounded conception encourages us to understand human life as lived within a limited time frame of a sentient, conscious being, ending with death. In contrast, a posthuman approach emphasises human becomings rather than beings. Lives do not end with physical death. Lives and deaths are intimately connected to their interrelations with non-humans, environments, machines and other humans. Digital legacies, for example, leave their traces of life in the online world. A family member never really dies in the familial stories that are told of that person for many years to come. This is a more affirmative view of death: where life is continuous. Braidotti (2013), 'posthuman critical thought does not aim at mastery, but at transformation of negative into positive passions' (p. 134). Boundaries between life and death have the potential to be blurred (see Chapter 9).

TOWARDS A DISHUMAN PERSPECTIVE

We have offered a summary of two philosophical positions: humanism and the posthuman. We write this book holding onto the pragmatic and the critical. We seek to critique humanism and offer alternatives though posthumanism. But we also want to keep hold of humanism: to seek a re-enchantment with this philosophy (Gilroy, 2018), to revise and revisit it in ways that emphasise the humanities of people who have historically been neglected by its promulgation. We are not done with humanism. Far from it, we acknowledge the political importance of human rights discourses and of the philosophical reaching out to disabled people to include them in this humanist discourse. But we are also energised by recent philosophical and scholarly ideas to extend humanism: to become posthuman. This straddling of humanism and the posthuman is an approach that we have defined as the DisHuman: which, we contend, simultaneously acknowledges the possibilities offered by disability to trouble, reshape and refashion the human (the posthuman) while at the same time asserting disabled people's humanity (humanism) (Goodley and Runswick-Cole, 2014). Our DisHuman approach which:

• Unpacks and troubles dominant notions of what it means to be human;

• Celebrates the disruptive potential of disability to trouble these dominant notions;

• Acknowledges that being recognised as a regular normal human being is desirable, especially for those people who been denied access to the category of the human;

• Recognises disability's intersectional relationship with other identities that have been considered less than human (associated with class, gender, sexuality, ethnicity, age);

- Aims to develop theory, research, art and activism that push at the boundaries of what it means to be human and disabled;

- Keeps in mind the pernicious and stifling impacts of ableism, which we define as a discriminatory processes that idealize a narrow version of humanness and reject more diverse forms of humanity;

- Seeks to promote transdisciplinary forms of empirical and theoretical enquiry that breaks disciplinary orthodoxies, dominances and boundaries;

- Foregrounds dis/ability as the complex for interrogating oppression and furthering a posthuman politics of affirmation.

(adapted from Goodley et al., 2018b)

CONCLUSION

In the remaining chapters of this book, we explore the ways in which disabled young people living with LL/LTIs articulated and defined their worlds in relation to some of the key themes of the dis/human: justice, celebration, intersectionality, dis/ableism, affirmation and desire. Most importantly of all, we do so as a diverse team of university-based academics and disabled young co-researchers. We do so in recognition that theory need not be the preserve of academics, but a collective and accessible endeavour whereby disabled young people's knowledges and lived experiences are central to theory building.

3

CO-PRODUCTION, PARTICIPATORY AND EMANCIPATORY DISABILITY RESEARCH

KIRSTY LIDDIARD AND LUCY WATTS MBE

ACCESSIBLE SUMMARY

- In this chapter, we talk about the role of young people in research.
- We think disabled young people should be research leaders.
- We talk about theories such as disabled children's childhood studies, crip time and how online spaces and virtual methods benefitted our project.
- We call for other researchers to use virtual spaces.

INTRODUCTION

I have been involved in other co-production projects but my involvement has never felt as fundamental to the project as it has in The Living Life to the Fullest Project. I feel a large part of this is the removal of boundaries and power imbalances – we are not a group of academics and co-researchers but rather a collective group with a range of experiences and theoretical knowledge and neither is more important. This has created an even playing field – no-one's contribution is more valid than another's and we have learned from one another.

– Katy Evans, Living Life to the Fullest Project Co-researcher

In this chapter, we add context to Katy's important words above – we detail the unique ways in which we have worked together as a project team of university-based academics and community-based disabled young co-researchers. In doing so, we detail the politics and practicalities of co-production. Co-production is now an established approach; however, as a diverse team we have developed inclusive research practices that engage with online and virtual social research methods in innovative ways. The use of the Internet has been argued to be transformative within social and educational research (Hewson, 2014). In Living Life to the Fullest, through virtual research environments, The Co-Researcher Collective has actively and meaningfully co-led inquiry – from the very beginning to its end. We centre such environments as highly beneficial to collaboration with one another, suggesting that social research technologies offer meaningful opportunities for valuing the embodied knowledges and lived experiences of disabled young people with life-limiting and life-threatening impairments (hereby LL/LTIs).

In this chapter, then, we offer a rare account of how inquiry happens in *practice* in co-produced projects (see Whitney et al., 2019). We begin by articulating a brief history of the location of non-disabled and disabled children in existing inquiry, and outline how our project embodies the politics of disabled children's childhood studies (Curran and Runswick-Cole, 2013; Runswick-Cole et al., 2017, 2018). We then move on to critically discuss The Co-Researcher Collective and its use of virtual and online research environments. We also attend to the dominant concerns around the 'extra time' required of researchers to undertake research with disabled young people. Using Alison Kafer's (2013) concept of crip time, we think through ways to reframe these alternative temporalities of research (see also Kuppers, 2014). Crip time is defined by Kafer (2013) as the recognition of (disabled) people's need for 'more time' – affirmation that diversity in embodiment and barriers in the social world means life can take place on a different timescale. As we detail the politics and practicalities of our processes, this chapter aims to encourage critical disability studies' researchers and others to take up virtual environments when researching with disabled people and undertaking empirical explorations of their lives.

INVOLVING CHILDREN AND YOUNG PEOPLE IN RESEARCH

Designing research that involves children and young people has burgeoned across the social and educational sciences over the last 20 years (Bailey et al., 2014; Clavering and McLaughlin, 2010; Hallett and Prout, 2003; James and

Prout, 1997). The politics of researching and consulting with children, both inside and outside of the academy, has undergone methodological and political shifts through a prominent children's rights discourse that has promoted an acknowledgement of children and young people as subjects-with-voice (rather than objects of study and intervention) and experts in and of their own lives (see Fargas-Malet et al., 2010; Kay and Tisdall, 2017; United Nations Convention on the Rights of the Child, 1989). According to Nind et al. (2012, p. 654), such shifts have emerged against the political and intellectual backdrops of the 'new sociology of childhood and moral and ethical standpoints about the importance of children's voices and children as social actors'.

Likewise, in a disability research context, emancipatory and participatory approaches (Oliver, 1992), which have emerged alongside disabled people's claims for civil rights, have (re)positioned disabled people as social actors with rights, and research as a potentially democratising activity aligned to disability politics with ethical approaches rooted in social justice and equity (Zarb, 1992). Research is positioned as inherently political (Swain et al., 1998) and as such has the potential to empower and/or exploit those who are its subject. In short, the traditional power relations inherent to academic research must be destabilised for inquiry to be in the interests of disabled people's emancipation. Thus, there are many overlaps and tensions between emancipatory disability research and child-led inquiry that are worthy of attention (Kellett, 2005b). It is important to note here that our project predominantly focussed on disabled young people, making it distinct from the contributions of researchers such as Kellett (2005b) who research with younger children.

More recently, emphasis has shifted towards the capacity of children and young people to act as researchers and partners in their own right who can contribute to inquiry in a number of ways (Bailey et al., 2014; Bucknall, 2010). Positioned as potential leaders of research that have 'an alternative, legitimate expertise to that of academic researchers' (Nind et al, 2012, p. 660), Bucknall (2010) suggests that such a shift is reactive to adult-centric histories of exploitative research upon children and young people. Thus, the notion of children as 'active' researchers in co-production contexts 'has been influenced by the perceived lack of children's own voices in research about their lives' (see also Kellett, 2005a, n.p.).

It is important to critically explore such shifts. While having good intentions, there is doubt as to the extent of democratisation of researching with children and young people, with critiques centred on tokenism; imbalances of power in child/adult collaborative research; and a denial of access to the full research process, with children and young people only being considered to have the 'capacity' to lead certain aspects of a project (see Coad and Lewis,

2004). Thus, while the role of the child in research has shifted significantly, it is noticeably still adults who hold much of the control regarding participation and research leadership. According to Kay and Tisdall (2017, p. 68), co-production and the inclusion of children and young people can in fact be used to 'control participation, to make service users complicit in experts' agendas'. Similarly, Carter and Coyne (2018, p. 171) stress that, to counter tokenism, being a participatory researcher means

> *a fundamental commitment to believing that children and young people can and will shape your research, construct and challenge your ideas and bring their own ideas and agendas to the table.*

Furthermore, discussion rests upon the specific roles of children and young people in the research process (Carter and Coyne, 2018). For example, some proponents of child-led inquiry argue that, inevitably, some aspects of the research process are better managed by adults (see Nind, 2008); for example, the writing up and publishing of research findings (Bailey et al., 2014; Nind, 2008). As Abell et al. (2007) state, it is academics that have the access to computer technologies, experience of academic writing and knowledge of peer review and publication. In the case of our project, the very book you're reading has been faithfully co-authored with and by co-researchers – we are sitting together writing this chapter type into our shared online document. Later in the chapter, we purposefully detail these methods of co-authorship (see Walmsley, 2004). As a team, it's a question we often get asked: but, how do you actually write *together*? Thus, our main focus in this chapter, of course, is not to debate whether disabled young people should be included in research, but to show *how* (see Tuffrey-Wijne et al., 2008): what we have learned from our experiences and how these can helpfully inform other researchers.

Where Are Disabled Young People in Inquiry?

In the last decade, public bodies – from non-governmental organisations to national charitable organisations – have begun to produce their own guidance as to how to research with children and young people. For example, the National Institute for Health Research (INVOLVE, 2016) developed guidance that stresses the importance of participation across the research process while being cautious of aspects of the research that might be 'too challenging, sensitive or inappropriate for children and young people' (INVOLVE, 2016, p. 3). Save the Children's (2000, p. 3) *Young People as Researchers* further questions the resources necessary to enact research relationships meaningfully. This particular guidance is built upon in the Joseph Rowntree Foundation's *Involving Young Researchers: How to Enable Young People to Design and Conduct Research* (Kirby, 2004), which argues for the early inclusion of young people into the process, alongside a political positionality that understands children and young people as vital contributors to health and social care research.

But where are the voices and expertise of disabled children and young people? Rabiee et al. (2005, p. 385) argue that, in general, disabled children and young people have been excluded from 'consultations and involvement in decisions which affect them' (see also Byrne and Kelly, 2015). This exclusion is echoed in research contexts, where disabled children and young people are less commonly involved in research than their non-disabled peers (Bailey et al., 2014). Thus, despite similar emphases in policy on the participation of disabled children and young people (e.g. see Every Child Matters, 2003; Children's Act, 2004), the disabled child and/or young person remains conspicuously absent, or at best marginalised, across research contexts, as well as in much of the practical research guidance referenced above, although there are some exceptions (see Bailey et al., 2014; Beresford, 2012; Nind et al., 2012). Our preliminary reading of such guidance reveals disability as present primarily only through concerns about safeguarding, accessibility and gatekeeping – a practical problem to *solve* – and thus that which demands extra time, resources and planning on the part of the academic researcher (see Bailey et al., 2014). Seldom is there any explicit focus towards disability as a worthwhile life experience and valuable lived perspective from which to contribute – a positionality readily adopted in The Living Life to the Fullest Project.

Interestingly, Bailey et al.'s (2014, p. 512) systematic review of 22 research publications that claim to have included disabled children and young people as researchers found that, across all studies, 'few details were given about involvement and limitations of involvement were not commonly evaluated'. Thus, little explicit information is often given in research write-ups as to what disabled co-researchers' specific roles are, or how these are enabled, encouraged or supported (see Littlechild et al., 2015). This is one of our key contributions in this chapter and book: to be clear about how The Living Life to the Fullest Project functioned as a co-produced project; how it made space for disabled young people to take control of the research agenda and methods; and, as Bailey et al. (2014, p. 510) put it, to 'define their own and others' roles in the project'. All Living Life to the Fullest Project co-researchers identify as disabled young women. It's important to note here that we have found very little literature that explicitly focusses on gender, co-production and research leadership (although there are quality exceptions – see Olsen and Carter,

2016). This makes our contributions in this chapter important towards thinking through the intersectional lives and identities of disabled co-researchers;
how class, race, age, gender, sexuality and nation – as well as impairment and
its effects (see Thomas, 1999) – impact participation, involvement and inclusion in contexts of co-production research.

Moving forward, then, it's pertinent to state that this othering is not new:
disabled children's childhoods have largely been omitted from progressive
moves to develop participatory methods for researching with children and
young people (Rabiee et al., 2005). Pluquailec (2018, p. 217) argues that the
participatory research agenda has overlooked the value of disabled children
and young people as worthy contributors to research, largely due to 'an overly
homogeneous conceptualisation of childhood agency' and an ambiguity
and lack of knowledge about how to mediate different types of impairment
within the research process. Thus, participatory methods with children and
young people are routinely steeped in ableist boundaries of what it means to
have and give voice and enact agency and autonomy (see Pluquailec, 2018).
Children and young people living with LL/LTIs – marginal lives at the centre
of our project – have been further marginalised: as research participants and
co-researchers (Gibson et al., 2014). Mitchell (2010) suggests that including
children and young people with LL/LTIs raises acute and often unexpected
challenges for researchers. Like Pluquailec (2018), Mitchell (2010) denotes 'a
standard approach' to research, where typical research tools are not diverse
or accessible enough to enable disabled children and young people to lead
or co-produce a project. Furthermore, Mitchell (2010, p. 1747) draws attention to a change in the pace of research where disabled children and young
people are involved: that 'listening to disabled children can take time and
negotiating access may involve a range of adults, not only parents/carers
but also professionals'. Olsen and Carter (2016, p. 6), who carried out co-
production research on rape and support with women with learning disabilities, noted that working in ethical ways with co-researchers 'took more time
than funders wanted'. They reported that each part of the project took several
weeks because of the extra time women needed to process information (Olsen
and Carter, 2016). Thus, while co-production research – inquiry that seeks to
embody equity, partnership and meaningful collaboration – makes attempts
to unsettle the problematic power dynamics inherent to academic research,
Olsen and Carter's (2016) experiences show this can often be compromised
by neoliberal academic and funding structures that restrict innovative and
equitable ways of working with marginalised communities. We come back to
this notion of 'taking too much' time in our explanations of crip time (Kafer
2013) later in the chapter.

THE CO-RESEARCHER COLLECTIVE: CONTESTING POWER IMBALANCES

The Co-Researcher Collective consists of six disabled young people (all women), most of whom live with LL/LTIs. However, despite our recruitment stressing the desire for diversity among co-researchers – with specific attempts made to recruit co-researchers with the label of learning disability and/or disabled young people from Black, Asian and minority ethnic backgrounds – all co-researchers recruited were disabled young White women from working class and middle class backgrounds (all but two have a university degree). This highlights co-production as a potentially exclusive research space that lacks diversity, even in the context of disability research (see Chapter 8 for how we tried to disrupt this).

However, we quickly found that the co-researchers we did recruit had a desire for social change and curiosity as to the potentials of social research:

The reason why I wanted to get involved in this project is because I feel that we have a duty to help young disabled people live their lives as they wish. To have experiences that, although are different and adapted from the experiences of our healthy counterparts, are just as rewarding – after all, we deserve that. Life is precious, let's live it to the fullest.

– Sally Whitney, Living Life to the Fullest Project Co-researcher

Importantly, in The Living Life to the Fullest Project participation and leadership was shaped and adapted to fit around the needs and wants of co-researchers. As such, much of our communication with The Co-Researcher Collective took, and still takes place, online – we connect daily through a closed Facebook group, Skype, FaceTime, email and Whatsapp. Far from embodying the tokenism that can plague research with disabled people (Liddiard, 2013), The Co-Researcher Collective meaningfully and authentically led the project, undertaking the majority of fieldwork, leading new routes through the project where needed, making key decisions and leading tasks across the research process.

Through virtual research environments, The Co-Researcher Collective actively and meaningfully co-led inquiry. To be clear (and to counter the poor reporting of young people's contributions in the literature detailed above), this involved: (i) supporting research design through discussion (planning both narrative and arts-informed approaches); (ii) co-writing interview schedules for participants; (iii) recruiting participants for data collection and carrying out online interviews through email, Facebook Messenger and Skype; (iv) planning the project's impact strategy and building relationships with impact partner organisations; (v) working with our community research partner organisations; (vi) meeting regularly to co-manage the research process as a whole; (vii) writing blogs and making films that communicate and document our processes and preliminary findings; (viii) presenting at conferences and research festivals; (ix) undertaking various public engagement and knowledge translation activities (both online and offline); and (x) co-authoring articles for publication, and now, (xi) co-authoring this very book.

RETHINKING METHOD/OLOGY

To proffer a brief overview of our methods, which we discuss throughout the book, in The Living Life to the Fullest Project we engaged primarily in narrative and arts-informed methods. In relation to the narrative, co-researchers carried out semi-structured interviews with 16 disabled young people (aged 18–35) living with LL/LTIs. All of these interviews were carried out using online technologies, primarily Skype, Google Meet, email and Facebook Messenger. Co-researchers undertook a collaborative form of research training with academic members of the project team, before recruiting, interviewing and maintaining relationships with participants.

In terms of our arts-informed approaches, we first hosted a residential Arts Retreat in 2017, led by disability arts organisation Purple Patch Arts (see purplepatcharts.org) with five disabled young men (18–25) living with LL/LTIs and their families. We purposefully invited siblings and families to come along; partly out of recognition that families provide considerable support for disabled young people, especially in residential contexts, but also that young people are embedded in families and associated intimacies that made their attendance more comfortable. The Retreat used the arts to tell stories – through a co-designed set of art-making practices, participants were able to speak of, relate to and articulate their experiences of living with LL/LTIs. Here's an excerpt from our project blog (Living Life to the Fullest Project, 2017, n.p.):

> The first day of our two-day Arts Retreat led by Purple Patch Arts
> has been action-packed. We are working with a brilliant group
> of young disabled people who are throwing themselves into the
> action without a second thought. So far, we've talked about what
> experiences and feelings we both hide and put on display through
> making lava lamps; we've made postcards of our happiest times and
> places; we've considered our heroes and what kinds of qualities are

important through a wall of words; we've thought about what's important in our lives – our relationships, aspirations for the future and what we enjoy – through making sand-mugs; and we've explored what we think of ourselves, but also the words and assumptions that get imposed upon us, through body-mapping. This latter activity was really interesting because it revealed that it's far easier to focus on the things we don't like about ourselves than it is the good. We know that this isn't just the case for young disabled people, but a whole host of groups: it's also endemic in a culture that proffers perfection and success as the only valuable ways to live. How might we change this? How might we celebrate each other and ourselves, and in ways that run counter to typical discourses of disability that only denote deficit, lack and burden? Most importantly, we have been documenting all of this with our Polaroid cameras (which are utterly awesome). It's been lovely to spend time with families, too. The Retreat being residential means that there's lots of time to have dinner together, play board games and chat into the evenings. Not surprisingly, families have similar stories about access, resources, services and provision, which reveal just how much fighting for what you and your family need has become the norm for many.

In 2018, we hosted two further arts workshops. The first was held at the Research Site 1 in Leicester, an arts centre that prides itself on being accessible and inclusive, with seven children and young people who had a range of impairments, including autism and learning disabilities. The second was at Research Site 2, which provides care and support for disabled children and young people, and their families, with eight young people living with LL/LTIs. The aim of the workshops was to enable disabled children and young people to tell new stories of their experiences of disability through poetry and spoken word arts. Sipho Ndopu, a spoken word artist and poet whose work explores disability, dyslexia and difference, led the workshops. In the workshops, Sipho worked in inclusive ways to co-create poetry with disabled children and young people based on their own lived experiences. The workshops offered quality arts engagement with inclusivity at its core. At Research Site 2 some participants came along in their hospital beds; participants labelled as 'non-verbal' participated through interpretation of support workers, through eye movements and through touch. Workshops acknowledged the ways in which mainstream arts activities and spaces can routinely exclude disabled children and young people, with the aim of building bridges between accessible arts and young people who aren't always afforded opportunities to participate. Following some fun warm up activities, young participants were invited to explore creative responses to questions such as: How do you see yourself? What do you like doing? What brings you joy? Colourful responses were offered through drawing, poetry, dancing, iPad play and performing for others.

Parents also came along to the workshops. At the Research Site 1, parents commented how special the centre is as a key resource for the family – a place to come for family time 'without being stared at'. Another parent said that she regularly brought her disabled child to the centre's coffee shop because it was a rare space in which they were welcomed, relaxed and included. These experiences emphasise just how difficult and hostile some public spaces can be for disabled children and their families. Furthermore, at the end of our workshops, we presented certificates to attendees, which many parents said was a rarity for their children.

The poems and artwork created across our arts approaches are powerful because disabled children and young people are rarely given space to express their thoughts, opinions and feelings, especially within the context of the arts. For us, the arts can generate a diversity of stories, countering the 'single story' of disability that routinely centres tragedy, particularly in the context of childhood. Thus, the arts can 'voice another storyline' of disability (Golden, 1996, p. 330) – one of joy, self-esteem and creativity – centring the lives of young people with LL/LTIs in this exclusion. Moreover, in The Living Life to the Fullest Project we consider disability arts as activism – creative storytelling with radical potential for disability rights and justice (Mingus, 2010b). As we found in our first Arts Retreat for young people living with LL/LTIs, art-making can provide a way to critically and sensitively reimagine the future as vital, desirable and pleasurable. We've found through young people's stories that many living with LL/LTIs are routinely denied opportunities to hope and dream 'future', despite the unremitting necessity to plan imposed upon them through the transition between child and adult care and services. The arts, when accessible and inclusive, can make space for this to happen.

COLLABORATIVE ANALYSIS: THEORISING TOGETHER

Our overall analytical approach in The Living Life to the Fullest Project is built upon an assumption that social theory can be generated through a meaningful engagement with a co-researcher group of disabled young people. Project co-researchers are theoretical provocateurs and theorists in their own right who, through their activism and writing, are reconsidering the meanings of life, death and disability. In short, co-researchers' contributions have been foundational to the theoretical development of the project. These critical contributions have meant that we are co-producing theoretical knowledges of the lives of disabled children and young people with LL/LTIs and their families. Co-researching has impacted on our shared theoretical thinking in relation to life, death and disability. While co-researchers have provided thoughtful counsel in relation to the methods and methodologies of the project, they have also offered their own perspectives through blogs and other multimedia resources that have had profound impacts on the theoretical work of The Living Life to the Fullest Project (see Liddiard et al., 2018).

Analysing the narrative and artistic data that came from a variety of data collection methods took place virtually (online) and through coming together at a residential Analysis Retreat, held in 2019. Co-researchers both physically attended the Analysis Retreat, hosted in an accessible hotel over three days, and joined us virtually. While we have prioritised virtual methods as a way to connect across the project, coming together in the same physical space added a depth and meaning to our analytical journey. We were able to sit together, in comfortable surroundings, to read through and discuss transcripts and co-researchers' experiences of engaging with the stories of others. For those who attended the Retreat, this was a very emotional experience.

Practically, we began with a Google folder in our shared Living Life to the Fullest Project Google drive containing all of the transcripts. Co-researchers accessed these for a few months prior to the Retreat to gain familiarity with the data in ways quintessential to qualitative analysis. Where co-researchers weren't able to read lots of transcripts, we would meet virtually to discuss key themes and participants' stories that were pertinent. We also hosted an online collective Analysis Workshop on Skype, which gave us the opportunity to come together as a team to discuss key themes prior to the in-person Retreat. Some co-researchers, who couldn't make the times of virtual meetings, sent in their thoughts in a Word document or email. Slowly, through working collectively on a shared Google document, we built a rough coding framework that was later developed at the Analysis Retreat. At the Retreat, we spent time reviewing transcripts in order to affirm the coding framework. Conversation was often emotional and intense, as co-researchers' own stories emerged through deep understandings of the stories of participants. This took time, but enabled the organisation of a lot of narrative data, before we began a broad thematic analysis that took place through sets of conversations about themes. For example, theme conversations included: family; living fully; independence; death and dying; future; sexuality, intimacy and relationships; friendships and loneliness; social lives; accessibility; equal opportunities; doing work; identity; media; illness and cure; relationships with animals; employment and education; and care and society's perceptions. Some of these themes fill entire chapters of this book.

From discussions within each theme, we explored the meanings of participants' stories to enable our key findings to emerge. Quite often, findings
emerged *across* themes. As an example, a central emphasis that disabled
young participants expressed across multiple themes was work and labour.
One of our key findings was that young people routinely carried out multiple
forms of work across the many spaces of their lives (see Chapter 7). This came
from a deep understanding of how young people spoke about the amount of
responsibility and labour organising their personal care could take; the emotional work they routinely carried out on themselves and others (e.g. managing parents' fear around their death); forms of identity work to 'come to
terms' with a disabled identity as a young person; self-advocacy and fighting
for access and services and so on. These are just a few of the forms of work
disabled young participants in our research told us they carried within their
everyday lives. Notably, while young people readily listed/articulated multiple
forms of work and labour, they didn't always acknowledge it as such, and
added to this, such labour and expertise was seldom recognised by professionals around the young person, and for many, their parents and families.

Slowly and collectively, word by word, we co-wrote our key findings at
the residential Analysis Retreat. This process took three days, but this was
partly because we needed to schedule regular breaks and periods away from
the room due to the physical and emotional labours of coding and analysing
data in the intensity of a Retreat. It's fair to say that much of this work was
experimental – we had little guidance or knowledge of how to collectively and
meaningfully explore data with our disabled young co-researchers. However,
we centred co-researchers' own engagements with the stories they had collected – What had they remembered? What surprised them? What was familiar? What forms of data haunted, scared, glowed, angered, resonated, excited
or confirmed? Because co-researchers had collected the very data we were
analysing, undertaking multiple interviews with their participants, building
relationships and learning about the lives and stories of others, they could
readily engage in such questions where analysis was, above anything else,
meaningful conversation.

EMBODIED KNOWLEDGE – VALUING LIVED EXPERIENCE

Engelsrud (2005, p. 281) argues that the 'researcher's body can be understood as both access and limitation to the acquisition of knowledge'. As such,
disabled people can offer a unique 'insider perspective' (Kellett, 2010) that is
critical towards furthering understandings of disability life and dis/ableism
(ableism and disablism) (Goodley et al., 2015), particularly the emotional

labours and affective politics of what it means to be disabled in such dehu-manising austere times (Runswick-Cole et al., 2018). This was echoed in our Analysis Retreat. In much the same way, co-researchers' networks enabled access to communities we may not otherwise have accessed, and their disabled identities and lived experiences of disability and dis/ableism informed the research process in immeasurable ways. As an example, many of the questions generated through discussion and later adopted in the interview schedules emerged from a deep (lived) understanding of what it means to live with LL/LTIs as young people with short/er lives. As interlocutors and co-constructors of participants' stories, co-researcher identity, subjectivity and embodiment became integral to the dialogical process of storytelling and our collabo-rative analysis. While we acknowledge that, at times, this required ethical considerations – both for prospective participants and co-researchers (and non-disabled researchers – see Goodley and Tregaskis, 2006), such questions have generated valuable and rich data for analysis.

According to INVOLVE (2016, p. 8), 'the importance of saying thank you […] should not be underestimated'. Thus, in order to not reproduce the exploitative relationships that characterise histories of research on disabled children – or invite the critiques of tokenism that some suggest may be inher-ent to research with children and young people (see Coad and Lewis, 2004; Kellett, 2005b) – we established a budget to fund co-researchers to purchase technology of their choice as recognition of their commitment and labour within the project. We note now, though, that on reflection this wasn't enough, and in all subsequent related impact projects to emanate from The Living Life to the Fullest Project we have paid all co-researchers at the hourly rates of a postdoctoral researcher pay grade for their expertise and contributions. We also invited co-researchers to become members of the research centre the Institute for the Study of the Human (iHuman) at the University of Sheffield – in acknowledgement that as researchers they should have access to research communities. We also offered co-researchers university certificates and refer-ences as evidence of their contribution of expertise, skills and knowledge to the project. This is important towards supporting the educational and work-based aspirations of co-researchers with LL/LTIs, the majority of whom face significant barriers to higher education and meaningful employment (Abbott and Carpenter, 2014).

VIRTUAL SPACES, DISABILITY RESEARCH AND YOUNG PEOPLE

The Co-Researcher Collective cannot have benefitted the research in the ways it has without access to virtual spaces and methods, often known more commonly as Internet-mediated research (Hewson et al., 2003), computer-mediated research or electronic research methods (Seymour, 2001). In an information age where new social technologies are rapidly (re)shaping human communication, online spaces can proffer new forms of inquiry: for example, netnography (Jong, 2017), web-based surveys (e.g. surveymonkey.com) and 'unobtrusive observation approaches' which 'gather data from existing online sources such as discussion group archives' (Hewson, 2014, n.p.). As Seymour (2001, pp. 147–148) argues, online and electronic research methods can 'substantially enhance the development of methodologies that relate more closely to the needs of research participants' and, we would argue, our co-researchers.

To 'draw disability in', many disabled people are often more visible online – where new forms of citizenship are being claimed due to the Internet (or 'online spaces') providing more accessible avenues for participation, communication, education, entertainment and employment than in the 'real life (RL) world' where significant barriers to these areas of social life forcefully prevail (Seymour, 2001). This digital access has been, for many, vital during the Covid-19 pandemic. Seymour (2001, p. 149) argues that information technology can serve to circumvent bodily function, 'enabling participation in previously inaccessible domains'. Others (Bennett and Segerberg, 2011; Pearson and Trevisan, 2015) have also suggested that online spaces (particularly new social technologies and social networking sites) offer new opportunities for social and political participation: access to rights, equity, justice and citizenship through disability activism, community-building and solidarity (see Obst and Stafurik, 2010), as well as raising a consciousness that has been particularly important to Disabled People's Movements through the austerity politics of past and present UK governments. Such technologies have also been integral towards enabling new avenues through which to fight for justice in response to the routine institutional violence and avoidable deaths of disabled people (see Ryan, 2017).

The Internet is also a platform upon which to build an identity of choice (Burch, 2016; Huffaker & Calvert, 2005): Bowker and Tuffin (2002, p. 340 in Burch, 2016, p. 8) suggest that this is because 'the power of the gaze becomes displaced by a textually oriented medium'. However, as in the 'RL [real life] world', ableism and disablism – key oppressions in the lives of disabled people – are ever-present. As Seymour (2001, pp. 148–149) reminds us, technology is far from neutral: 'old forms of social division underpin the new information age'. Thus, it's important to not homogenise the disability experience in relation to virtual technologies – digital exclusion remains a key form of oppression for many disabled people (Lane-Fox, 2010; Watling, 2011). Digital exclusion is exacerbated as more and more of our lives 'move' online in what Watling (2011, p. 491) calls 'visions of a digital future': banking, food shopping, community-building, activism, social communication, finding friendship, love and intimacy and accessing sex (Liddiard, 2018a). Adults with the label of learning disability, people with visual impairments and D/ deaf people are routinely excluded and Othered in online and textual media – it is likely this has contributed to the lack of diversity in The Co-Researcher Collective. Furthermore, as conditions of dis/ableism have become more acute through the austerity agenda of multiple UK Governments, hate speech and crime, both online and offline, have worsened 'propagating a metanarrative of disability as the ultimate "dustbin for disavowal" within a climate of austerity' (Burch, 2016, p. ii; see also Burch, 2021).

Despite this, disability researchers have demarcated online or virtual research environments as being of significant value to existing and emerging disability research methodologies (Bowker and Tuffin, 2004; Carr, 2010; Liddiard, 2013, 2014a; Seymour, 2001; see Obst and Stafurik, 2010) – for myriad reasons. Firstly, they are often malleable to different embodiments, capabilities and bodily functions (although, as we suggest above, this has its exclusions). Secondly, virtual arenas can offer greater accessibility and privacy: new social technologies can provide the means for disabled people to participate in research without this becoming known to social workers, personal assistants, carers, partners and parents. Thus, for disabled young people with LL/LTIs, who face significant exclusion in multiple spaces of their lives (Abbott and Carpenter, 2014) – often aggravated by their need for complex medical care, support and interventions – online spaces can offer improved access to social, political and cultural worlds. Yet, Seymour (2001, p. 159) argues that in the context of a disability research agenda, '"giving a voice" means more than providing the researched (and, we would add, co-researchers) with an opportunity to speak: it involves creating the appropriate means and communication context'. Although, as Nind (2008) stipulates, the idea of some people empowering others raises particular questions, making this positionality of giving/claiming space and voice a key tension in co-production. We suggest, however, that our online research relationships with one another as researchers in The Living Life to the Fullest Project embody our egalitarian research politics as well as counter the routine dis/ableism inherent to the research process: we actively work towards generating a politicised space that welcomes and values the perspectives of young people with LL/LTIs (see Chapter 7 for a more detailed analysis of our collaborative working). Markedly, this is facilitated through the ways in which the Internet 'erases boundaries of time and distance' (Eysenbach, 2001; n.p.) and blurs public/private divides, meaning that our relationships as colleagues are not restricted to neoliberal temporalities of 'work'. Some disability theorists have called this 'Crip time' (Kuppers, 2014), defined by Kafer (2013) as the recognition of (disabled) people's need for 'more time' and a political acknowledgement that contexts of ableism propagate timescales and temporalities that benefit non-impaired bodies and minds. Crip time was a powerful notion for all of us in the team; Co-researcher Katy expresses it beautifully:

> *Crip time isn't a concept I've experienced in any other work. It has enabled me to work around my capabilities and in turn, become more aware of looking after my health and fatigue levels which has had wider benefits than my research work. The expectation is we know what we can manage so I don't feel the shame I've felt in other work when I've needed some time out or the pressure to push myself to the max to prove my worth. I feel working in this way has enabled me to contribute more to the project as I've been able to do it when I feel well enough rather than forcing myself to do something when my mind and body are screaming no. This has kept my love and enthusiasm for the project high.*

In relation to The Living Life to the Fullest Project, then, online environments mean our project invites flexibility with regard to time. Through the intricacies of crip time (Zola, 1998), new temporal frameworks of research embody alternative orientations in and to time. For example, we messaged at all times of the day and night; we scheduled meetings around the presence and time of care visits and support from personal assistants; Skype meetings involved breaks to adjust tracheostomy tubes or seat cushions; blog posts and tweets were written during the night; online interviews via Facebook Messenger were meticulously broken down into multiple sessions due to exhaustion on behalf of the interviewee and/or the co-researcher; contributions required regular breaks due to frequent hospitalisations; and planning a 'physical get-together' (e.g. to a conference) took considerable time and labour due to the need to manage multiple barriers to access. We do not mention these here as negative impacts of impairment, but as vital moments to rethink and reconsider conventional temporalities of qualitative methods and research processes. Rather, once again we suggest that these embodied experiences shaped the process to the benefits of our participants – disabled young people with LL/LTIs and their families – ensuring that the materialities of disabled body-minds are centred in inquiry, rather than written out and overlooked. In our project, impairment is more than an 'unwelcome presence' (Shildrick, 2009, p. 32), but serves to disrupt the embodied norms of inquiry, acknowledging the generative relations of alternative ways of being in the research process.

In this way, our processes became more responsive to the real life worlds of disabled children and young people with LL/LTIs and their families.

DRAWING SOME CONCLUSIONS

In this chapter, we have detailed our experiences of some of the politics and practicalities of co-producing disability research as a diverse team of university-based researchers and disabled young co-researchers. We have made attempts to locate the disabled child and young person in 'child-as-researcher' discourses, movements and literatures, demarcating their routine exclusion and marginalisation – particularly in the context of LL/LTI. Our experiences articulated through this chapter highlight significant gaps in the literature here that a focus on the disabled child-as-researcher does not offer enough towards thinking about the possible roles and leadership of disabled young people in and across research contexts and its possibilities for their futures. Moreover, where disabled young people are positioned as researchers, far more practical and explicit information needs to be written into research studies in order for young people's contributions to be fully acknowledged, rather than merely the negative emphasis of the 'extra time and labour' facilitating their participation can take academic researchers.

As a means to show the value of disabled young people's participation and co-leadership of the research process, then, we have articulated the work of The Co-Researcher Collective. Through discussing our successes and failures, we have centred accessible virtual research environments and online spaces as that which, in the case of our project, enabled us to welcome diverse embodiments, levels of skills and knowledge and enable meaningful leadership on the part of disabled young women co-researchers – who are often shut out of leadership (Liddiard, 2018). We recommend, then, and encourage other critical disability researchers (and others) to embrace social research technologies. This is due to the very ways in which they can offer opportunities for valuing the embodied and unique 'insider' knowledge (see Kellett, 2010) and lived experiences of disabled people as researchers and participants, as well as incorporating the flexibility of crip time to research processes that are typically dominated by normative neoliberal frameworks, temporalities and body-minds (Kafer, 2013; Kuppers, 2014). Thus, virtual spaces, we argue, are critical to the ethical development of collaborative disability research with young people, particularly those with LL/LTIs.

In sum, as our experiences detailed in this chapter reveal, what is required to democratise research with children and young people (disabled or not) is a shift in what constitutes research 'contribution', 'capability' and 'leadership' – the notion that enabling leadership and control of the research agenda by non-academics involves challenging the normative (and ableist) rubrics of research and its traditional methods to give better access to researchers with a wide range of skills, capabilities and knowledge. Lastly, as we have attempted in this chapter, we call for researchers who practice co-production to better map their empirical experiences of research as a key way to develop existing inclusive research methodologies towards the potential contributions and values of marginalised young people as contributors and research leaders.

4

POSTHUMAN CONNECTIONS: RETHINKING ANIMAL–HUMAN RELATIONSHIPS

KATY EVANS, SALLY WHITNEY-MITCHELL AND RUTH SPURR

ACCESSIBLE SUMMARY

- This chapter explores co-researchers' and participants' experiences of having an assistance dog.

- An assistance dog is a term for a dog that provides assistance to a disabled person, and is trained to provide support.

- We explore these connections between animals and humans.

- We conclude that care from animals is deeply valuable for disabled young people.

INTRODUCTION

The Living Life to the Fullest Project has affirmed our interest in posthuman disability studies. This approach has enabled us to consider the promise and potential of humanist and posthuman epistemologies, theories, methodologies, interventions and activisms (Whitney et al., 2019; see Chapter 2). Whilst humanist formations are predicated upon a bounded, rational, autonomous and sovereign human subject, the posthuman condition suggests something more expansive, relational and nomadic (Liddiard et al., 2018; Braidotti and Regan, 2017). As a research team made up of disabled young co-researchers and academics, we engaged with a DisHuman approach to theory and activism (Goodley and Runswick-Cole, 2014). Our approach blends the pragmatics of humanism with posthuman possibilities. It is also open to the connections, in this case trans-species connections, that can be formed. A DisHuman approach holds in place two perspectives: the disrupting posthuman work done by dis-ability in the world (the Dis of the DisHuman) and continued importance of embracing a humanist philosophy that recognises disabled people as fully human (the Human of DisHuman). This means we acknowledge that many disabled young people – co-researchers and participants – *desire* key elements of humanism: independence, autonomy and rationality. However, our engage-ment with their lived experiences has shown that their lived realities embody many posthuman possibilities. In this chapter, we use disabled young people's intimate engagements with assistance dogs as an example of how the blending of animal and human incorporates the posthuman values of interdependence, mutuality and reciprocity.

To embody some of this theory, we look at what that means for disa-bled young people living their lives in partnership with assistance dogs. We centre on impact research that emerged from The Living Life to the Fullest Project – The Canine Care Project (Whitney et al., 2020). The Canine Care Project was a small piece of research, designed and led by co-researchers, that explored the experiences of disabled young people who have assistance dogs. We partnered with Canine Partners, a registered charity that changes the lives of disabled people through partnering them with assistance dogs. We did so because early findings from The Living Life to the Fullest Project showed that assistance dogs can play a significant part in the lives of disabled young people and can transform their experiences of living with disability. For example, young people told us that an assistance dog did far more for them than practical tasks (although these are very important), but actually made them feel happier, safer and more at ease in social situations. The Canine Care Project, then, began with a desire to explore these findings further. As Co-researcher Ruth explains:

> My assistance dog Willow's work isn't just about all her incredible tasks, it's also about the confidence she gives me and others, the belief in myself, the ability to go out and be independent, and be safe and as always, a conversation starter with anyone I meet.

In the first section of this chapter, we explore the connections that are made possible between animals and humans, through a posthuman lens. We focus on interdependencies, identity and inclusion in young people's own stories.

Later in the chapter, we look at the ways animal–human relationships can offer multiple forms of emotional support to disabled young people, in ways they say benefits their mental health and wellbeing (Whitney et al., 2020). We also investigate the mutuality in caring relationships between disabled young people and their assistance dogs.

This chapter contains a multiplicity of voices: we share findings from The Canine Care Project, stories from The Living Life to the Fullest Project and intersplice this with co-researchers' own lived experiences of human–animal partnerships. Specifically, Katy and Sally each lead their own sections of this chapter, integrating their own experiences into the stories of others. We conclude the chapter by suggesting that canine care is a transformational and deeply valuable form of care and support for disabled young people. We argue that there should be more research about, and awareness of, the ways in which interspecies relationships are a fundamental element of rethinking future human relationships, especially for those who are marginalised and displaced.

LOOKING AT CONNECTIONS WITH ASSISTANCE ANIMALS FROM A POSTHUMAN LENS

Posthuman approaches emerge as a response to the fixity of classical, modernist and humanist conceptions of the human (Liddiard et al., 2018). For Braidotti (2013, p. 159), 'this new knowing subject is a complex assemblage of human and non-human, planetary and cosmic, given and manufactured, which requires major re-adjustments in our way of thinking'. It is this new way of thinking about subjectivity in terms of assemblages that we see reflected in the lives of disabled young people where the amalgamation of biology/technology is 'intimately and complexly entangled in relationships with other humans and non-humans; a globalised entity of virtually infinite proportions' (Braidotti, 2013, p. 37).

Human beings often define themselves in terms of their abilities: 'the ability to speak, to act, to create, to think, to feel, to be self-aware, to exercise free will' (Saur and Sidorkin, 2018, p. 6). This is humanism and those that cannot enact these abilities risk being excluded (Saur and Sidorkin, 2018). Historically, humanism has embraced some humans and constituted others as sub-human or in-human through slavery, categorisation, institutionalisation, demonisation and marginalisation. It can be seen from this that defining someone's status as human in terms of their ability may directly impact many disabled young peoples' sense of worth and lead to further marginalisation and ultimately a feeling of rejection by society. We are concerned with the ways in which, under this ideology, those who are deemed valued subjects tend to coalesce around the same kinds of human – namely 'able' and economically productive – and argue that this can exclude disabled young people.

Yet, we have found that humanism remains a key guiding philosophy associated with finding oneself a place in the world for several of us co-researchers in The Co-Researcher Collective (see Goodley et al., 2014b). This is hardly surprising when much of what we understand as cultural politics is undergirded by humanist and ableist ideas. A number of co-researchers use the language of humanism in order to affirm their own sense of self; as Sally reflects (Liddiard et al., 2019: 1478):

> *In February 2012, I was diagnosed with another rare genetic*
> *condition – Ehlers-Danlos syndrome. There was no cure. In my*
> *previous healthy life, everything that I had wanted I was able to*
> *achieve by pushing hard and working at things until I got to the*
> *place I wanted to be. I adopted the same methodology to overcoming*
> *my illness. I had to decide how I was going to get to Edinburgh to*
> *study medicine. I think I still thought that I could push through and*
> *do things on my own, through hard work, as I'd always done.*

The need to claim our individual worth (a humanist concept) as disabled women – who have historically been written out of humanist discourses – is understandable. Yet, we do not simply stay within a humanist realm. Whilst still emphasising our human(ist) characteristics, we as co-researchers with assistance animals have also described the potentialities invested in our nested relationships with other humans and non-humans: as assembled selves connected with and to non-human others, in our case, canines. Braidotti (2013, p. 71) describes the connections between humans and animals as vital interconnections, positing a 'qualitative shift of relationship away from speciesism and towards an ethical appreciation of what bodies (human, animal, others) can do'. She highlights that this posthuman position requires the 'displacement of anthropocentrism and the recognition of trans-species solidarity' (Braidotti, 2013, p. 67), something that we co-researchers very much agree with as we discuss the blurring of our human–animal bodies in the remainder of this chapter (Liddiard et al., 2018).

ASKING QUESTIONS ABOUT INTERDEPENDENCIES

It was this insight into the importance of animals (and specifically for us, assistance dogs) in our lives as disabled young people that led to our decision to include questions about assistance animals in the interview schedule that we co-designed for interviewing participants in The Living Life to the Fullest Project (see Chapter 3). Only two young people we interviewed had an assistance animal. However, for those who did, their description of living life as a disabled young person in a relationship or partnership with a canine was described as deeply transformational. The stories young people told of how their assistance dog impacted their lives, and the passion with which they spoke about this subject, was incredibly powerful. We were struck by some of their profound declarations:

> Sam: *Making sure she's ok is a reason for me to make sure I am ok – I look after myself better so that I can look after her as she deserves. People treat me differently too, they ask about the dog rather than asking why I'm in a wheelchair*

> Imogen: *I feel safe and brave [with assistance dog Olive], and we are starting to explore new opportunities. (Canine Care Project Participant)*

It is from these rich and often surprising stories that we can begin to understand that trans-species relationships are deeply important to disabled young people and that these partnerships (or posthuman assemblages) powerfully impact their lives, hopes and aspirations for the future. Price-Robertson and Duff (2016, pp. 61–62) describe an assemblage as 'conceptual mélanges of the material and the discursive whereby texts, discourses, bodies, affects, technologies, non-human 'things', and physical and social contexts combine'. The very idea of an assemblage seeks to address the oftentimes superficial and artificial distinctions between the real/ideal, material/immaterial, object/subject, human/non-human and digital/physical. Applied to the human being the concept of the assemblage recognises from the very outset that humans are deeply complex hybridised non/human phenomena. We are organic, digital, technological, environmental, social, biological, animal, human, economic and cultural political entities; now more than ever. Indeed, the Covid-19 pandemic has demonstrated beyond doubt that the human condition is deeply dependent upon a coexistence with animals, machines, environments and other humans. This contemporary human condition has been described as posthuman (Braidotti, 2019): a mix of human and non-human interrelations and connections. Disabled young people are, we would argue, at the forefront of these considerations. They are the quintessential posthuman subject (Goodley et al., 2014b). For example, young people's stories we collected have emphasised the following:

- The positive emotional impacts of canine support.
- The emergence of new intimacies between humans and animals.
- The ways in which assistance animals contribute to the building of positive identities and futures.
- How assistance animals can transform the social lives and experiences of disabled young people with life limiting and life-threatening impairments (hereby LL/LTIs).
- The new found independence stemming from these interdependencies.

It is clear that the relationship between an assistance dog and a disabled young person is even more powerful than we previously imagined and than has been described in disability studies literature, which has seldom included animals because of its Marxist and materialist roots (see Chapter 2); although there are some notable exceptions where theorists have discussed their relationships with animals (Michalko, 1999; Taylor, 2017). Therefore, in order to more fully understand the impact of these relationships, we undertook a small impact project called The Canine Care Project (Whitney et al., 2020).

The aim of the project was to further explore how building intimacies with assistance dogs affects disabled young people. It required us to collect further data from disabled young people and we decided to do this in two ways. Firstly, through our Living Life to the Fullest interviews we had collected a good amount of qualitative data. Additionally, our charity partner, Canine Partners had also generated personal case studies from their human-partners, which we thought were valuable narratives to include and we had full permission via Canine Partners from the story-tellers to do so. To offer some more scope and breadth, we decided to collect some additional quantitative data to get a better measure of the impact of assistance dogs and administered an online questionnaire to disabled young people (aged 18–35) who are partnered with an assistance dog from Canine Partners. Once we had analysed the results, we began to see how much our existing qualitative data reflected the experiences of *many* young people. It was clear that assistance dogs are in profound relationships with our disabled young participants. Co-researcher Ruth describes a multitude of tasks her dog undertakes:

> *Willow assists me inside the home; like helping with undressing, washing, picking up dropped items, fetching named items, opening and closing doors, fetching the post, passing notes between myself Mum and the carers and lots more.*

It is important to point out that there are many different kinds of assistance dogs with a variety of roles and associated taskwork. Our research primarily focussed on disabled young people with physical impairments who had assistance dogs to support them with everyday tasks. Outside of the physical help assistance dogs provide, we explored eight specific areas of disabled young people's experience with their assistance dogs. These included: independence; social inclusion; relationships and emotional support; emotional wellbeing (including mental health); care; physical wellbeing and safety; motivation, confidence and embracing new challenges and meeting expectations (Whitney et al., 2020). These were the areas of impact that we measured quantitatively, but from The Canine Care Project we learned so much more about the effect of posthuman connections in disabled young people's lives, which we have explored elsewhere in the context of posthuman disability theory (Liddiard et al., 2018). Moreover, several of these themes opened up new areas of exploration for us as co-researchers; challenging us to consider how assistance dogs have changed our feelings of self-worth and relationships with and to our own disabled identities.

In the following sections, we offer co-researchers' own first-hand accounts of the meanings of these partnerships within their lives. We do so to articulate the complex narratives that can surround autonomy, independence and care for disabled young people.

INDEPENDENCE, IDENTITY AND INCLUSION: CO-RESEARCHER SALLY AND ASSISTANCE DOG ETHAN

The data from other disabled young people made me consider even further the life-changing and identity-shaping effects of having my own assistance dog and what my relationship with my disability was like prior to our partnership. Before getting Ethan, I forcefully rejected my identity as a disabled young person. I was striving to prove myself as an independent, autonomous adult who was in control of her own life, future and capable of meeting all my own needs. From a disability studies perspective, it would be fair to say I was desperate to define my worth from the humanist viewpoint of being able (as described earlier by Saur and Sidorkin, 2018, p. 6) – because that is how I believed I would prove my value. I lacked purpose; I couldn't see how I would ever become a meaningful member of society again. My life-threatening condition was so complex and hard to diagnose that I was often met with disbelief and the assumption that it must be in my mind. As a result, I didn't believe that I was of value to anyone. I refused to entertain the idea that this was the rest of my life. I was constantly fighting against my body, against my disability and fighting to rid myself of the identity of a disabled young woman. This rejection of my disability was brought to a head after suffering such a severe seizure that I stopped breathing. From that point on I started to receive 24 hour care and use a wheelchair full-time. I could no longer ignore my disabled status but it was not something I relished. Yet, taking the step of applying for an assistance dog meant that I had to face the facts of my own *limitations*. But somehow, acknowledging the things that I couldn't do on my own, but that a dog might do for me or with me, seemed a positive step forward.

Partnering with Ethan has proved more than a step forward. It has changed the way I live my life and how I view and accept my own disability. Ethan brings freedom from the oppressiveness that requiring 24 hour care, for some, can bring. He allows me an independence in the home that I otherwise wouldn't have. My carers do all of the required tasks for me but achieving them on our own, between me and Ethan, brings a fabulous sense of freedom. Ethan has proved invaluable at keeping me safe and allows me to be in rooms on my own without the need for constant checks to make sure I'm OK. He can use a bell to ring carers, he runs to get help from a carer by nudging them and leading them to me. He is able to recognise symptoms of a seizure or collapse before I'm aware of them and will alert me to them and then get help. He is trained to lie next to me whilst having a seizure.

Independence

As summarised elsewhere (Whitney et al., 2019), the blurring of human–animal bodies (in my case, my own, Ethan's, and to some degree, my power wheelchair) reflects a posthuman way of approaching the world and has allowed me an independence that would have not otherwise been possible. Paradoxically, I have garnered this independence from my *interdependence* with Ethan and my wheelchair, and this has had a huge impact on me and my relationship with my disabled identity.

Independence is one of the strongest themes that has emerged from The Canine Care Project (Whitney et al., 2020) and runs through each area of life we explored. For example, most disabled young people stressed that their assistance dog has generally made them more independent (87.9%) (Whitney et al., 2020, p. 6). Jay described the impact of his Canine Partner leading him to move into his own home and states that the reason for moving

> is to give me more independence and start a new chapter in my life as I'm now 25 years old … [my assistance dog] gives me the confidence I need to know that I'll be fine on my own. (p. 33)

In fact, it is impossible to pull out independence as a theme on its own as it emerges in every aspect of living in partnership with an assistance dog.

Indeed, we as co-researchers strongly identify with this positive impact as well, despite independence being considered an ableist rubric that denotes the broad cultural logics of autonomy and self-sufficiency (Whitney et al., 2019). Yet, independence is something that is of huge importance to disabled young people as it is something we found in our primary research, The Living Life to the Fullest Project, that has often been routinely denied for much of their lives. The relationship I have with Ethan, and that of our other co-researchers' and their assistance dogs, are not just a technology for enabling (humanist) desires but (provide) a posthuman intimacy that offers expansive ways for living (see Whitney et al., 2019). Therefore, paradoxically, we co-researchers celebrate the independence that directly results from interdependencies with our assistance dogs.

Interspecies Relationships and the Emotional Support They Provide

Living as a unit with Ethan addresses some of the very real aspects of living with a disability and further illustrates how the boundary between Ethan and myself is blurred: I previously felt isolated and misunderstood by my non-disabled counterparts. Yet now, I no longer have any time when I feel alone or isolated. I always have my trusty side-kick who loves me and believes in me no matter what. His unconditional love and constant desire for cuddles is a treatment in itself! Working towards new tasks with Ethan has gone a long way to giving me back that need for industry and a sense of purpose.

From The Canine Care Project (Whitney et al., 2020, p. 39), we discovered that almost all disabled young people (98.3%) said their 'assistance dog was like a friend to them' and 87.9% went so far as to say that their 'assistance dog was like a significant other'. Such intimacies are echoed by one participant, Tash who said, '... through both the good and bad days, [canine partner Cuthbert is] my rock and my support through life. I would be so lost without [him]'. I would go so far as to say that the intimacy I share with Ethan has meant he has become a part of me (or maybe we are a part of one another). We are an assemblage, a melding of human and animal. This is echoed by Jay from The Canine Care Project (Whitney et al., 2020, p. 6) who says, 'the bond between us is strong, it's almost like he's an extension of me'.

In public places, Ethan and I are an entity together and are perceived totally differently from myself on my own. The questions from others that would previously focus on my disability, the pitying glances I would receive or even the feeling of invisibility have all disappeared, and instead are replaced with admiration and curious questions about my handsome Canine Partner and the instigation of real, adult conversations surrounding him and the help he provides. Discussion shifts from the negative aspects of my ill health to the incredibly positive asset of having an assistance dog. People stop me in the street to comment on Ethan as opposed to how sad it is to see a 'young, attractive' woman in a wheelchair. I am visible again, more confident to present myself and more part of society. Interestingly, Co-researcher Katy describes the power of her assistance dog not seeing or knowing her labels:

> *Folly doesn't see the labels placed on me by others, the*
> *preconceptions these bring or the many negative stereotypes*
> *disabled people have to wade through. Folly just sees me. Through*
> *the confidence Folly has given me I have developed a stronger voice*
> *and I expect to be accepted by others because Folly has shown me*
> *it's possible.*

Faith, from The Canine Care Project, said their dog 'has helped to show everyone the real me' (Whitney et al., 2020, p. 28). This in itself is an interesting concept and raises many questions about why having a dog seems to put non-disabled people at ease enough to allow them to get to know us on a deeper level, rather than through the preconceptions that society teaches them to hold. For Katy, this led her to not only accept herself but also changed her expectation of how the rest of society should see and accept her.

Social Inclusion

Wonderfully, 'Ethan and Sally' as an assemblage has meant that we now are more able to relate to and socialise with other humans. Moreover, Ethan's presence has impacted those around me and their ability and confidence to relate to me. In The Canine Care Project (Whitney et al., 2020, p. 28), Faith also experienced this:

> *I have always wanted to have the confidence to know that I can*
> *influence my own world and allow people to see me rather than*
> *just my condition. [Now] when out and about with Ted, I feel that*
> *people are talking to me as my own person and seeing me rather*
> *than treating me just as someone who has cerebral palsy and is in*
> *a wheelchair. My confidence has grown so much … Ted has helped*
> *me to show everyone the real me!.*

It seems that the stripping away of the labels and preconceptions of others via the medium of assistance dogs leads to a reduction in social isolation. As Co-researcher Katy says:

This is something I experienced following two years of feeling socially isolated at university. Once I had Folly people approached me much more. Folly provides a bridge between the well-known experiences of dog ownership and the largely hidden world of disability through which people began to get to know me better.

Co-researcher Ruth describes a similar experience whereby her dog Willow becomes a much needed icebreaker that non-disabled people need to interact with her:

Before Willow, people would just ignore me. Being in a wheelchair is difficult enough, in addition to the feeding tubes, venting tube, catheter and central line sticking out my chest and stomach. I was so used to feeling isolated, cut off and invisible to the world. But with Willow that's no more. Everyone warms to her and wants to say hello. They see her working and they want to ask questions, then, before you know it, they've realised I'm just a normal young woman in my 20s, like anyone else. I just happen to be in a wheelchair and have some tubes to do the jobs my body doesn't. But that doesn't define me. I'm so much more than that. People just have to take the chance to get to know me and with Willow by my side they now do.

EMOTIONAL WELLBEING AND MENTAL HEALTH: CO-RESEARCHER KATY AND ASSISTANCE DOG FOLLY

To explain the emotional impacts and mental health benefits of having an assistance dog, we share Living Life to the Fullest Co-researcher Katy's experiences, which explain the unexpected impact of her connection with her Canine Partner Folly on her emotional wellbeing. In this section, Katy focusses on grounding and responsibility as key themes that enhance her emotional wellbeing. Katy intersplices her lived experiences with findings from The Canine Care Project (Whitney et al., 2020).

The Canine Care Project (Whitney et al., 2020) highlighted a direct connection between the partnership with an assistance dog and a disabled young person's emotional wellbeing and mental health. This is seen clearly in Rachel's description of how her assistance dog supports her and the difference this has made to her wellbeing (Whitney et al., 2020, p. 6):

During my training course with Eve I laughed more than I had ever laughed before and the heavy weight I had been carrying lifted.

I started my final year at university feeling much more optimistic with Eve by my side. I often felt lonely and homesick at university and it was very reassuring to wake up every morning to Eve's brown nose and waggy tail.

The improvements in emotional wellbeing and the hope instilled by a canine partnership was explicit in young people's stories, as Rachel further stated (Whitney et al., 2020, p. 25):

I was losing interest in everything I had previously loved. This all changed when I went down to Canine Partners [Headquarters] to meet a dog they had in mind for me. ... In that instant she stole my heart and something came alive inside me again.

Mainly focussing on the benefits of the physical tasks my Canine Partner Folly could do meant I initially underestimated the impact on my mental health, but for me this has been Folly's biggest benefit. During our partnership, I have had two mental health crises and I believe it is largely thanks to Folly that I have made it through. It may seem contradictory that I attribute my mental wellbeing to her despite the years of our partnership being the most mentally challenging. This is because Folly has given me the confidence to face trauma I experienced in the past through trauma therapy, and has been by my side throughout this difficult journey. The following are examples of Folly's support, along with findings from The Canine Care Project (Whitney et al., 2020), which support our assertion that assistance animals can provide disabled young people with exceptional forms of emotional support.

Grounding

Dogs live in the now. Whilst I recognise this statement as somewhat anthropocentric, I want to emphasise that when so much of disabled life feels uncertain and overwhelming, dogs can offer their humans an important reminder to take things moment by moment. Co-researcher Ruth has actually learned how to live better *from* her dog. She encourages us to remember:

Dogs don't need much .... They remind you to focus on the simple things in life, the little things. Yes look at the big picture too but don't get overwhelmed. Sometimes just stop and be in the here and now with them. Enjoy the little things around you like they do; go on those walks with them, watch them running around having the time of their life with their tails wagging and tongues out.

Whilst they run, look up at the blue sky, see the birds fly, hear them tweeting away. Feel the fresh air and wind blowing past your face. In those moments I've learnt to 'be more Willow', to take a deep breath in, close my eyes and just embrace that moment.

In times of great anxiety, Folly has learned to rest her head in my lap which reminds me I'm safe and not alone. This has been essential to counteract flash-backs as well as making me realise connecting with another being is safe and extremely healing. Being suspicious about the motives of people and whether they can be trusted is something I struggle with due to past traumas. Opposed to humans, Folly is straightforward; she does not have any hidden agendas and I think this is what has allowed me to build the greatest level of trust I've had with any other living being. Folly represents safety and security to me; I always know where I am with her. When I start getting ahead of myself wor-rying about all the things I cannot control, Folly giving me a ball to throw reminds me to stay in the now. She has shown me that laughter really is the best medicine.

Reciprocity

Folly depends on me for her survival. When I am struggling, the need to feed, exercise or simply love Folly keeps me pushing forwards despite how I'm feeling. Disabled people often experience high levels of unpredictability from fluctuating health to personal assistants (PAs) being suddenly unavailable which can significantly impact our mental health and place us in a constant state of alertness. Folly has relatively simple needs and her routine is comfort-ing when life feels overwhelming. At my worst, I struggle to care for myself because I don't feel I deserve it but the need to care for Folly forces me to look after myself too.

In The Canine Care Project (Whitney et al., 2020), 86.2% of disabled young people identified with this sense of responsibility and 60.2% said that their assistance dog had helped them take better care of their physical health. In fact, participant Sam explained:

[...]making sure she's [assistance dog Blue] OK is a reason for me to make sure I am OK – I look after myself better so that I can look after her as she deserves.

This caring responsibility also challenges the notion that disabled people are only cared *for* which has increased my confidence and balanced out the feel-ings of being a burden on others (see Chapter 7).

CARE AND CARING: CO-RESEARCHER SALLY AND ASSISTANCE DOG ETHAN

Katy's acknowledgement of the burdens of being cared for chimes with my own experience and those of the disabled young people in The Living Life to the Fullest Project, as does her description of assistance animals providing the feeling and actions of a reciprocity of care. The Canine Care Project (Whitney et al., 2020) Shelly revealed sometimes resenting needing support from other people:

> *I didn't want to have another adult, carer or PA with me all the time, not that there's anything wrong with that, but I'm very independent and always try to be as independent as possible. (Whitney et al., 2020, p. 35)*

Before I had Ethan, I was 100% reliant on human care which led me to feel incredibly vulnerable: it is hard to have so many needs that can only be fulfilled by another person. I was having seizures far more regularly and my health was incredibly unpredictable. I was in and out of hospital (Resus and Intensive Care). Apart from God, and my parents who birthed me, I didn't have anyone by my side who would be with me through thick and thin. A human carer or PA is ultimately there to do a job and is being paid, which means the power relationship between carer and the cared for can be incredibly complex and difficult to negotiate. This imbalance took away my sense of independence and self-assurance.

Ethan and I are able to understand and respond to each other's needs in ways that alleviates the constant emotional pressure that can be part of receiving care as a disabled person. Importantly, 81% of participants in The Canine Care Project (2020) agreed with this sentiment. Receiving care as a disabled young person can involve considerable emotional labour. Emotional labour is described as the performances of emotion we are expected to give in certain situations (Hochchild, 1983; Liddiard, 2014). For example, participants in The Living Life to the Fullest Project often talked about having to show gratitude upon receiving care and support from others, even if they did not feel it. For me, this included feeling guilty about my constant needs, apologising for them or worrying about the strain on my human carer, especially family members. When relying on a close relative for care, the dynamic of the relationship can change. Interestingly, Sam (a participant from The Canine Care Project) explains that there can even be discomfort on the part of others when a disabled young person is cared for by a human:

> *Seeing Blue [Canine Partner] pick up something I've dropped or tug off my jacket is funny and cute and adorable, people love watching*

*it; having another human do the same thing makes people feel sorry
for me or feel sorry for the person helping me. People love watching
an assistance dog work but can be uncomfortable watching another
person provide care and assistance.*

This is a fascinating insight that highlights the real complexity in the
dynamic of care provided by humans and how the assemblage of dog and
human caring for one another can dramatically change this, not only for the
disabled person, but for others too.

Physical Wellbeing, Safety and Vulnerability

In addition to the immense impact an assistance dog can have on a disabled person's mental health, as Katy described in an earlier section, we also
found that assistance dogs can have significant impacts on the ways disabled
young people engage with physical health, as Co-researcher Ruth explains:

*One of Willow's tasks, which she wasn't specifically trained for, is
that she can now detect when I am going to have a blackout due
to my POTS (Postural Orthostatic Tachycardia Syndrome). She has
learned to do this by detecting my scent and how it changes when
I'm unwell. This has been incredibly beneficial, not just to me, but
to my family and carers too, as I am now able to do things more
independently knowing Willow is by my side. She can give me a
2–3 minute warning before I am going to pass out so I can
then take my medication, lie down and get to somewhere safe.
Previously, I could and would injure myself easily, so I needed
someone with me 24/7 and we were all constantly on edge.*

Ruth also alludes to the measure of safety and reassurance that this brings
not only to herself but also her loved ones:

*Willow keeps me safe. She quite literally saves me from daily
injury and gives me independence like I never had before. Most
importantly, my loved ones can now breathe a little easier knowing
I have my four-legged warning system with me, alert to look after
me wherever we go.*

It is clear to see once again that from this trans-species intimacy that independence has been regained. The care Willow provides for Ruth surpasses that
of human care in some ways as it relies on Willow using a level of smell that
humans do not possess. This incredible ability to use their initiative to better
support people was further described by Tash: 'Cuthbert has taught himself
how to help me push [my dislocated joints] back into place, this isn't something

he was taught at Canine Partners' (Whitney et al., 2020, p. 38). It is another example of what can be achieved through embracing intimacies with non-human beings. Ruth also highlights the safety and security an assistance dog can provide, not just to the individual with whom they are partnered, but for their wider family and friends too. Affirming this notion, The Canine Care Project found that over 93.1% of disabled young people feel less vulnerable at home, and 96.6% feel less vulnerable when out in public (Whitney et al., 2020).

MOTIVATION, CONFIDENCE AND EMBRACING NEW CHALLENGES

As reported in The Canine Care Project (Whitney et al., 2020), disabled young people state that their partnerships with their assistance dogs have impacted their sense of purpose and zest for life. These posthuman connections have encouraged disabled young people to set new goals (87.9%) and try new things (84.5%), including getting into education and work. Disabled young people also overwhelmingly reported that having an assistance dog is an effective tool for coping with the difficulties of life that can come with disability, by changing their outlook and motivation (Whitney et al., 2020). Co-researcher Katy describes the taking on or sharing of difficulties as 'one subject' with her assistance dog: No one knows what the future holds but when I'm doubting myself it's hugely reassuring when Folly nudges me with her nose and I'm reminded we are facing whatever challenges may come together.

We also suggest that the increased sense of motivation resulting from the partnership with a canine comes about from the increased sense of self-confidence that having an assistance dog can bring (Whitney et al., 2020). Rachel explains:

> Eve's [assistance dog] unquestioning acceptance has allowed me to accept myself and given me so much confidence. I recently landed my dream job of being an advocate for young disabled people.

This clearly reflects the interplay of our other findings where a sense of acceptance by an assistance dog directly affects the self-worth, confidence and understanding of identity for disabled young people themselves. Ruth describes Willow's acceptance of her and what this means:

> No matter what's going on in your life, what you're wearing, what you're doing, what day you've had; they never judge you, will always love you, always forgive you and look to you for guidance, which gives you a focus and purpose.

Co-researcher Sally feels: this self-acceptance comes from Ethan becoming a very real part of *my* identity. He has challenged me to re-address my self-worth and value to society. Once again, the tension in my self-identity between needing to be 'able' and 'of value' to the world and that of recognising that I am not only a valuable subject when autonomous, is founded from humanist and ableist roots (Braidotti, 2013). However, as someone who has felt stripped of independence and control over my life, embracing an assembled self has changed my outlook. Prior to Ethan, due to the disbelief and punitive treatment I received in hospital, my self-worth was incredibly low. Ethan challenged me to believe that I could be of worth to someone else. It was this realisation that led me to have the confidence to start dating and begin to see myself as desirable. My previous notions of having no worth were overturned by Ethan's reliance on me and things we could achieve together. This gradually impacted my self-esteem and allowed me to embrace my disabled identity. This self-propelling, symbiotic relationship meant that I could imagine myself in other meaningful roles, contributing to my community and being of value to others. And so began my foray into the world of volunteering, public speaking, media appearances and academic research. As we have reflected elsewhere (Whitney et al., 2019), it is through these human–animal-technology assemblages that our co-researchers get a place at the humanist table. Yet, I see now that the need to be seen as desirable to a romantic partner and the rest of the world (a humanist recognition) was a mask for a deeper seated need to accept and believe in myself for who I am. Co-researcher Ruth is able to describe how living in an assemblage with Willow not only affects her 'now' but also her ability to consider the future:

Before I got Willow I was really struggling to see hope beyond my illness, my hospital stays and my time back and forth to intensive care. I wasn't living, I was just surviving. Willow gave me hope again, gave me a purpose and a zest for life that had been lost for so long. I struggle a lot with my mental health. When living with a life threatening illness you never know what tomorrow may bring and facing life threatening situations again and again really takes its toll on you emotionally and mentally. Some days it really did feel like 'well what's the point anymore?' Then Willow came into my life and reminded me there is always a reason to smile, always a reason to get up and face the world, always a reason to have hope.

The hope that Ruth describes above echoes many of the voices of disabled young people in The Living Life to the Fullest Project. Living life with a LL/LTI can be hard and the challenges are often numerous. However, the disabled young people we interviewed do live full lives and, for many, this is aided tremendously by connection with an assistance dog (Whitney et al., 2020).

CONCLUSION

In this chapter, through the stories of disabled young people we have explored the connections that are made possible between animals and humans. Young people have shared their own perspectives on how interdependencies with animals can have positive impacts for their sense of identity, inclusion and emotional wellbeing. In the context of human–animal relationships, disability illuminates the tension between our sovereign and assembled selves, something that we all experience in different ways across the lifecourse. One of the gifts of disability is its disruptive potential to acknowledge such tensions and celebrate our interdependencies (see Chapter 2). Most importantly, however, we have shown the extent to which animal–human relationships can offer multiple forms of emotional support to disabled young people, in ways they say benefit their mental health and wellbeing (Whitney et al., 2020). Much of this emotionality is based upon a mutuality of care, a reciprocal love and a shared partnership in life. We argue, then, that canine care is a transformational and deeply valuable form of care and support for disabled young people. We believe that the posthuman connections between co-researchers, participants and other disabled young people with assistance dogs have a lot to teach the world about how to live and what it means to be human. As such, we strongly advocate that there should be more research into, and awareness of, the ways in which interspecies relationships are a fundamental element of rethinking future human relationships, especially for those who are marginalised and displaced.

5

DISABILITY AND FAITH

SALLY WHITNEY-MITCHELL AND KATHERINE RUNSWICK-COLE

ACCESSIBLE SUMMARY

- The focus of this chapter is on disability and religious belief.

- It draws on the personal experiences of the chapter author and of three participants in the project who talked about the importance of faith in their lives.

- The chapter argues for the importance of faith in the lives of disabled people and the need to acknowledge this more widely.

INTRODUCTION

This chapter responds to the lived experiences of disabled young people with life limiting and life-threatening impairments (hereby LL/LTIs) and their experiences of faith and religion. We begin the chapter by outlining the complex relationship between critical disability studies and the studies and practices of religion, which goes some way to explain why this aspect of disabled young people's experience is so often missing from discussions about their lives. We then move to draw on the experience of Co-researcher and lead author of this chapter, Sally Whitney-Mitchell, who reflects on her journey of illness, disability and faith and on her discussions with Becky (this participant requested to use her real name), Helen and Josh, participants in the project and disabled young people for whom faith has become an important part of what it means to live life to the fullest. We conclude the chapter by reflecting on the importance of religion in young people's lives and we call for a greater openness to conversations about faith and religion within critical disability studies and beyond.

'DISABILITY STUDIES NEEDS MORE RELIGION' (IMHOFF, 2017, P. 186)

In responding to Imhoff's call for 'more religion' in disability studies, we want to pay attention to two things: the structures and social practices of religions and the meanings of faith in the lives of disabled young people. Traditionally, British disability studies have been shaped by Marxist materialist concerns with the structural barriers disabled people face creating the conditions for exclusion and oppression: the social model of disability (Oliver, 1990). Marx (1843) was, of course, highly critical of religion, which he famously described as 'the heart of a heartless world' (pp. 53–54). Religion, for Marx, functions as a pervasive allusion, it distracts one from the suffering of now, by creating a grandiose, greater sense of sin and virtue and causing those who suffer to believe it is at fault of their own sinful indiscretions. For Marx (1843), religion is the 'sigh of the oppressed creature'. Following Marxist thinking, by making a simple division between activists and the institutions of oppression, materialist social model thinkers have typically rejected both medicine *and* religion as oppressors of disabled people (Claassens et al., 2018).

It is not surprising that disability studies scholars have recoiled from an exploration of the meanings of faith and religion in the lives of disabled people. Imhoff (2017) notes that religion is often absent in introductory texts to disability studies; she cites Davis (2010), Goodley (2011) and Titchkosky and Michalko (2009) as examples where religion is missing from their seminal critical disability studies texts. Indeed, Imhoff (2017) argues that disability studies have not only ignored religion, but have often taken a hostile stance towards it. She admits that religions have been seen to be complicit in marking people as 'abnormal' but she rejects what she sees as critical disability studies' construction of religion as something that only 'hurts people with disabilities' (Imhoff, 2017, p. 186).

While British disability studies have failed to engage with faith, studies of religion and theological studies have, on the other hand, often engaged with disability. In religion and theology, disability is, often, very present, usually represented as something having 'gone wrong' with individual bodies and minds (Reynolds, 2012, p. 17). Indeed, this identification of something 'gone wrong' is often exploited as an opportunity for religions (Reynolds, 2012). In the Christian tradition, for example, disability is characterised variously as: 'a cross to bear'; an opportunity for God 'to heal'; an opportunity for non-disabled people to demonstrate charity as they comfort themselves with the prayer 'there but for the grace of God, go I' (Reynolds, 2012). Some have used the words 'holy innocents', 'God's little ones' and 'the poor' (Reinders, 2012, p. 36) found in, but not attributed to, disabled children in the Bible. And the birth of a disabled child has often been described as a punishment from God (Chataika, 2012). Moreover, religious experience has often been conflated with mental illness (Schutz & Gyula, 2018). It is not, then, surprising that religion might be regarded as hurtful to disabled people and their families. An appeal to religion involves navigating, yet again, the construction of disabled people as 'other'. In these secular times, when faith is characterised as irrational, a turn to faith may also seem to be a risky strategy for improving the lives of people who are already often positioned as lacking reason and independence (Goodley, 2014). And yet, a turn to religious institutions can bring with it the cultural capital accrued by members of faith-based organisations (McKinnon, 2017).

Looking beyond the UK, faith and disability are, of course, global issues. Across the globe, disabled people are just as likely as their non-disabled peers to have faith (Disabilities and Faith, 2016). Globally, religion and faith is of central importance in many people's lives and so, by rejecting religion as only a form of oppression of disabled people, disability studies fails to engage in a multiplicity of narratives about religion that act as crucial reference points in disabled people's lives (Chataika, 2012). The experiences of disabled people of faith have been underrepresented in disability studies and so, here, our aim is to recentre people of faith within disability studies scholarship and activist communities (Claassens et al., 2018). We follow a tradition within disability studies scholarship of addressing the exclusion of marginalised groups [see e.g.: Chappell et al.'s (2002) work with people with learning difficulties; Beresford's (2004) work with mad identified people and Slater and Liddiard's (2018) call to include trans people in disability studies debates].

In order to centre the experiences of disabled people of faith, we are drawn to the work of academics from Europe and North America who have engaged with disability, albeit primarily from the lens of religious studies and theology, rather than starting with a critical disability studies perspective. In 1994, Nancy Eisland published *The Disabled God;* this was followed by the founding of the European Society for the Study of Theology and Disability and a disability group within the American Academy of Religion (Reinders, 2012).

Building on its emergence as an inherently intersectional inquiry, we think that critical disability studies is enriched by seeking moments of (inter)connection across disciplines, including theology and religion. And while disability studies academics in the global North have been quick to dismiss charity models of disability, which are lazily elided with religious models of disability, as demeaning to disabled people as the 'less fortunate' (Goodley, 2011), scholars from the global South have offered more sustained and nuanced engagements with religion and disability (Chaitaika, 2012; Claassens et al., 2018). They have, perhaps, been forced to pay attention to the lived experiences of disabled people in contexts where access to education, employment and social participation are made possible by the presence of faith-based organisations (Claassens et al., 2018). However, in a climate of ever deepening austerity, and as a result of the Covid-19 pandemic, in contemporary Britain, we too see evidence of faith-based organisations providing support to people living in poverty, which includes many disabled people (EHRC, 2016).

PUTTING FAITH AT THE CENTRE

In the next part of this chapter, in our attempts to centre disabled young people's experiences of faith and religion within studies of disability, we present Co-researcher Sally's first-person reflections on her personal journey with illness, disability and faith, which includes conversations that she has had with another disabled young woman, Becky and a couple, Helen and Josh, as part of the wider research project.

Sally's Journey with Illness, Disability and Faith

The consideration of religion as an institution that oppresses disabled people and forms yet another structural barrier to exclude marginalised people, discussed above, is one that clashes with my own lived experience of religion and Faith. I use the word Faith here and throughout with a capital 'F' to describe my belief in a divine power as opposed to use of the word 'faith' that describes having faith or trust in something generally. Instead of experiencing exclusion and marginalisation, I have found great relief, a place of peace and a way to cope with the challenges and anxieties of life with my disability through my Faith as a Christian. Perhaps, even more radically, I have met a God as a person with whom I can identify and a set of beliefs and a way of living that does much to include all, especially marginalised people. The development of this relationship, and this ability to rely on an infrastructure founded in Faith in a God of immense love, has provided me with a way to live my life and go forward.

My journey of illness and disability has been a very difficult one of great personal struggle and pain. I have had to work hard at accepting and then embracing disability but, I believe, this has only been possible due to my Faith and reliance on God. The God that I know may not fit into the traditional and sometimes archaic understanding of Christianity and the Church, but the relationship I have with Him (I do not believe that God has to have a gender but I will hereupon use the pronoun He/Him) is very real and I believe is reflective of an all-loving God that can be found through all aspects of life and time.

My lived experience of Faith and disability has become intertwined with how I experience and understand the world. Here, I focus on how my journey of illness, disability and God has led me to understand hope, suffering, faith and love, and is central to my living a full life.

Hope and Suffering

Hope is central to my life; hope is what gets me through my struggles. But what may seem difficult for others to understand is that what has brought me to hope is suffering. My personal journey has involved a great deal of suffering. It might, at first, seem odd to focus on suffering in the context of a book which is driven by young people's hopes, dreams and aspirations and the positive contributions they make to their communities, but suffering is a very real experience in my life. It features in the lives of many of the disabled young people we have spoken to as it does in the lives of non-disabled people; it is not unique to disability but a part of being human. But, for me, and many of others, talk of suffering is not incompatible with discussion of hopes, dreams and aspirations. Through suffering there have been positive outcomes; suffering has transformed my relationship to disability, and in the presence of God's unerring love, suffering has brought me to hope. Josh, echoes this view when he describes how his life is 'shaped by hope' and he believes suffering is 'at the heart' of Christianity because 'Christ suffered'.

This never-ending hope, that I have held closely to me, must come from somewhere. I truly believe it has grown from pushing through, holding on to hope even as I suffer pain after pain, and loss after loss. I have carried on. The Bible says 'we [a] also glory in our sufferings, because we know that suffering produces perseverance; 4 perseverance, character; and character, hope.

5 And hope does not put us to shame, because God's love has been poured out into our hearts through the Holy Spirit, who has been given to us' (Romans 5: 3-5). So, if all this suffering has led to God's love literally filling my heart, then is it possible to say the suffering that has started this chain is something to glory in? I know that if I had lost all hope at any stage of this journey then I wouldn't be the person I am today and I genuinely doubt that I would be alive.

In our discussion of Faith, Becky, said that:

> If I didn't have my Faith then I don't think I would see my life like I do now, and I might feel hopeless as living with disability is so hard, and it can feel like it is one battle after another.

Josh also describes how the hope he has, stemming from his Faith, changes the way he sees his life with a disability:

> before I knew God my disability kind of made me feel down and sad a lot of the time, but now, even though it does get me down sometimes, overall I have lots of joy and a lot of peace and a lot of Faith.

Becky goes on to explain how this hope has real, practical implications on her life:

> Someone without a faith would not have the hope and assurance that I have about God's love, His peace, hope for the future and His help with day to day life.

For me, God, as I know Him, is suffering right along with me. I believe that He knows my pain and my torment, not only that, but He actually embodied suffering love and demonstrated it in all its painfulness as Jesus when he was crucified on the cross. As a disabled young person, to have a God at the centre of my world, who comes alongside me and shares in my struggle, and in whom I see my journey reflected, is revelatory and life-changing. I find solidarity with a God who truly knows my pain, experience and suffering. It is a stark contrast to a world that views my life from a distance and which defines me as other, broken and ultimately someone to whom it is impossible to relate. And it is here that I find restoration, not from disability or imperfect bodies, but from our self-imposed separation from God. Society views and judges me for my deficits and impairments, the things I cannot do. But with Jesus I am made whole – my suffering has driven me back to God. C.S. Lewis (1940, p. 3) described it in this way: 'God whispers to us in our pleasures, speaks in our conscience, but shouts in our pain: it is his megaphone to rouse a deaf world' (though we recognise his own ableism in the metaphor of a 'deaf world').

INTERDEPENDENCY AND VULNERABILITY

Disabled people, people of colour, migrants, homeless people, older people and countless other minoritised groups have been constructed as vulnerable. During the COVID-19 pandemic, the risks imposed on the lives of those made 'vulnerable' in society accelerated as the politics of vulnerability turned into a politics of disposability, where some lives mattered less than others in the fight against the pandemic (Ossei-Owusu, 2021). And it is here that I believe that study of Faith in the light of disability can help us to think differently about vulnerability; not as a property of minoritised individuals, but as a point of connection for us all. The crucified Jesus portrays a world where it is not all about perfect bodies (in His case, it is a scarred bleeding one) or autonomous individuals but an acceptance of one's vulnerability, interdependency and the welcoming of marginalised people. This belief embraces the fact that we as humans cannot function as self-reliant entities and the realisation that admitting this and looking outside of oneself (to God and to others) can be a source of great strength.

This resonates with the work that we have been doing on the project in which we, as a group of disabled young women co-researchers, have worked together as a collective (see Chapter 3). We recognise and value our interdependencies and, for me, this interdependency is informed by my connection to God.

Here, the cross over is apparent again. Braidotti (2013, p. 37) recognises it when she seeks to move beyond what she describes as 'lethal binaries' to find different ways of thinking about the human subject as relational and interdependent. She contends that occupying a posthuman position requires a disengagement from narrow, normative visions of the self to become, instead, 'relational in a complex manner that connects it to multiple others' (Braidotti, 2013, p. 167). In the project, we have seen the many interdependencies that are formed between co-researchers, disabled young people and their carers, family members and even trans-species with assistance animals (see Chapter 4). It is here that the notion of 'self' is most disrupted by both disability and an understanding of the world that depends on a relationship with God.

Occupying a posthuman position requires: 'the knowing subject disengaging itself from the dominant normative vision of the self' (Braidotti, 2013, p. 167). This disengagement and reliance on self is urged in the Bible too: 'You will not succeed by your own strength or by your own power, but by my

Spirit', (Zechariah, 4:6) says the Lord' – so that the subject becomes 'relational in a complex manner that connects it to multiple others' (Braidotti, 2013, p. 167). This echoes our relationship with God that is described in the Bible, where over many passages it describes how we are found in God and He is found in us (e.g. 'God lives in us and his love is made complete in us' (1 John 4:12)). These frequent reassurances of our intimate connection and indwelling by God demonstrate the nature of our interconnectedness and how through this relationship we develop potential, identities and understanding that are impossible singularly. As Nicky Gumbel (2020, n.p.) states when reflecting on Ephesians 1 1-23, 'Understanding that, as a Christian, you are "in" Christ revolutionises how you see yourself, your self-image, your identity and how you understand your value to God'. Verse 11 of this passage states: 'It's in Christ that we find out who we are and what we are living for' (v.11, MSG). As Josh describes, it is this relationship that gives 'a purpose for my life, it isn't just to be here and suffer and die, it's here to know God, to know Jesus'. This describes how the model the world uses to assign worth (this may be material blessings, non-disabled bodies, power) is vastly different to God's (since it is through Him that we find out what we are living for) and when we adopt His perspective then we truly find our value. In posthuman times, *both* disability and theology emerge as moments of relational ethics that demand an understanding of ways of being in the world beyond independence and autonomy (Goodley et al., 2014b).

Faith is central to my life and has helped me to reshape my beliefs about my own vulnerabilities. The fact that I know a God who is vulnerable, not ashamed of his frailties (as the human, Jesus) and is willing to join me in the place where I am, a place of immense vulnerability, helps me to understand my disability and to embrace it. There is something very affirmative about the description of Jesus after his resurrection; he didn't return as a wholly healed and bodily perfect being. He came back to us with his wounds from the crucifixion still in place, he was scarred (John 20:27).

To be clear, I don't believe that I am broken any more than any non-disabled person or, in fact, anybody else. I do believe that my position in society, as a marginalised disabled young woman has led me to reflect on my own life and recognise the vulnerabilities I carry. As a 19 year old who was bedbound, unable to move, helpless and completely reliant on others (and consequently most open to abuse), it was at this very time that I became closest to God and He seemed more present in my life. Disability scholars may take issue with my description of my vulnerability and infer that I see myself (and other disabled people) in the same way as Western society seems to view me – as one of the 'losers' of society.

My understanding of vulnerability is very far from that, and joyously, my Faith helps me to reframe that belief. Rather, God came for the broken and he came for the weak but not because those who perceive themselves to be strong and self-sufficient (by society's standards) need Him any less but because He meets us in our place of marginalisation and redefines what it means to be 'weak'. Williams (n.d., n.p.) states that: 'the concept of weakness is seldom used in a physical sense in Scripture'. God has empowered me to own my supposed 'weakness'.

Moreover, I, Sally, an oppressed and seemingly powerless disabled young woman, *look* like the broken Jesus (metaphorically, not just because my body too is seemingly broken) and by being in that same position I have the opportunity to more easily draw close to God – not relying on worldly standards and status to find my value. Becky also describes how her Faith has changed how she considers her life with vulnerabilities:

> *I pray to God every day and ask Him to help me. I also read*
> *the Bible. Sometimes in the things I read or hear, it helps me see*
> *situations in my life differently or makes me feel about them*
> *differently.*

Helen also discusses how her disability has made her more aware of her weakness and changed her relationship to vulnerability, saying:

> *There are additional kinds of special weaknesses that come with*
> *having a disability. The reality is, me and Josh cannot be left alone,*
> *we are physically vulnerable for example ... but it's also true that*
> *everybody has emotional weaknesses and internal weaknesses,*
> *which are more important to be honest, and it's not helpful to hide*
> *from that. I think society in general needs to start talking about its*
> *weaknesses.*

Helen's empowerment, which comes from facing her vulnerability head on, is shared by her partner Josh when he says:

> *being reminded of my weaknesses ... (as) it's not very easy to hide*
> *my difficulties. ... That's helped me to draw close to God and be*
> *like 'help me with this'.*

Josh demonstrates that, with God, there is strength in weakness and much to be gained: 'human weakness is not a liability only because it makes room for the power of God' and a dependence on Him and, I would argue, an interdependence with others.

A posthuman orientation requires us to rethink interactions between humans and non-humans on a relational and 'planetary scale' (Braidotti, 2013, p. 6) and to embrace 'collectively shared, community-based praxis' (Braidotti, 2013, p. 100), as an 'accountable recomposition of a missing people' (Braidotti, 2013, p. 100). Goodley et al. (2014b) argue that this posthuman approach fits with the tenets of critical disability studies, but we can also see that it fits with the tenets of religious thought.

As evidenced, Christian traditions cause us to embrace relationality and vulnerability. As Reynolds (2012, p. 21) argues:

> *Viewed through the lens of basic vulnerability, 'neediness' or 'lack of ability' is not a flaw detracting from an otherwise pure and complete human nature. Rather, it is testimony to the fact that we – all human beings – receive our existence from each other.*

And we would go so far as to argue, we receive our existence and identity from God too and this is the way that we can embrace our disabled identities and positions in a posthuman world. The ability to look outside the norm, outside of the idea of perfect bodies and pride in autonomy and see the beauty in diversity, to learn what God looks like, to know God's love and to recognise the love of God in others reflects my journey of embracing my disability through Faith.

LOVE, 'OTHERNESS' AND THE MARGINALISED

The power of God's love is that He transforms the way we see others and redefines who the 'other' is. It is here again that we see the power of how Faith reflects what we discuss and argue for in disability studies. Delio (2011, p. 61) discusses the globalised bias we experience today sees 'immigrants, welfare recipients, incarcerated, mentally ill, … disabled, and all who are marginalized by mainstream society' as a problem. Indeed, Becky adds that: 'Sometimes I think that it is other people who have a harder time accepting my disability and including me as an equal person'. Some theologians have called for an end to a theology premised on the bifurcation of 'us and them' by 'thinking theologically about ourselves in ways that eliminate the distinction between people with and without disabilities' (Reinders, 2012, p. 35). Many working in critical disability studies have also troubled the politics of 'us' and 'them' (Overboe, 1999; Runswick-Cole, 2014). Delio (2011, p. 61) questions this othering that stems from fear and explains that in so doing we cut ourselves off from God:

> When we reject our relatedness to the poor, the weak, the
> simple, and the unlovable we define (those whom are considered
> to be God's children) ... over and against God. ... Because of our
> deep fears, we spend time, attention, and money on preserving
> our boundaries of privacy and increasing our knowledge and
> power. We hermetically seal ourselves off from the undesired
> 'other', the stranger, and in doing so, we seal ourselves off from
> God.

Richard Rohr (2016, n.p.) states that the God he and I know came into this world 'as a homeless baby in a poor family, then a refugee in a foreign country, then an invisible carpenter in his own country which is colonized and occupied by an imperial power, ending as a "criminal", accused and tortured by heads of both systems of power, temple and empire ... and finally buried quickly in an unmarked grave', surely an embodiment of the 'other'. For me, by assuming this identity, God truly aligns himself alongside the marginalised and undesired and in so doing disrupts the normalised order and hierarchy of society in a revolutionary way. So, when we open ourselves to God, we also open ourselves to the undesired stranger and vice versa. Not only that, but we redefine the 'undesired stranger' as someone not so different from ourselves, or in this case 'me'. This ability to bring together those that are seemingly so different (for me, those who live in bodies that are non-disabled, often male, and don't face the barriers I do daily) is a refreshing and extraordinary feat.

And I would argue that if others can see God in me – a disabled young woman or 'other' – then they are able to accept God's love; a healing love that leads to embracing the 'other'. God's very presence can be found in the world that He created that is full of limitations and pains. His presence is not found in spite of this weakness but because of it: 'the priority of God's love (is) in weak, fragile humanity' (Delio, 2011, p. 61).

Indeed, *I* am a weak, fragile and, from the world's perspective, 'broken' young woman and yet God's love can be found in me. But this is not to say that I subscribe to the medical model of disability and see myself as any more broken or in more need of repair than anyone else. The world as I know it seems to decide 'who is worthy of our attention and who can be rejected ... in place of God' (Delio, 2011, p. 61). Yet, when we accept 'created reality with all its limits and pains (and that includes everyone and everything equally) we see the living presence of God in our world' (Delio, 2011). We are all equally weak and broken but, joyously, I have discovered we are all equally loved. It is not because God doesn't see my disability but His love seeks out suffering and shares in it and then lifts us up to share in this union.

FINDING SELF-WORTH AND IDENTITY THROUGH FAITH

Returning to the idea of identity developed through Faith, I look back at my life and see how through my struggles I felt my old life was being wrenched away and I was desperate to retain it. However, here too I was able to learn from God's love in relation to my disability and how I see the world. In John 15: 1-2 it states that:

> [...] my Father is the gardener. He cuts off every branch in me that bears no fruit, while every branch that does bear fruit he prunes so that it will be even more fruitful.

This describes the process of 'pruning' (the cutting back, reshaping or even dying of the old to make way for something new or better) as a way to bear fruit. This concept is found in all of nature and many other belief systems. Josh describes how seeing people in the Bible 'being tortured and dying for their Faith' was pivotal in his understanding of pruning and how God can use suffering 'to transform us and to shape us'. Josh admits that 'it's not always pleasant ... but God achieves it in making us more humble people that are reliant on him'.

For me, seeing the loss of this previous, non-disabled life as an act of reshaping or 'pruning' and thereby allowing the emergence of a new life has been so helpful for my acceptance and then embracing of my new state of being as disabled. Moreover, further fruit has appeared in my life. One of those fruits has been my partnership with my assistance dog Ethan from Canine Partners (see Chapter 4). Despite being in a situation I could not previously have imagined, living with incurable conditions, 24 hour care and life-threatening symptoms, I found myself in a place where so much good has happened that my understanding of my disabled identity has been reborn. My match with Ethan (a perfect match, one which could only have been orchestrated by the creator of the Universe) has transformed my life and showed me that I no longer had to reject the notion of my own disability. Ethan's unconditional love for me means he doesn't see my illnesses, my weakness, my flaws, he just sees me, Sally, and there is freedom in that. Moreover, God *does* see these things and accepts and loves me. In fact, Ethan also helps me to reframe my disability and changes it from a negative thing. He helps me to accept my illnesses and embrace my weaknesses (I note here that the bible uses the word weaknesses and I will too. But I don't mean weakness that I need to be ashamed of or that I bear the blame for. I define weaknesses as the difficulties I have in my life and have to carry), which has led to new realms of life opening up for me bearing fruit. I would never have met Ethan if my life had not turned out as it has and if I hadn't undergone vigorous pruning.

Other young people also describe how their Faith has changed their understanding of their disabled identities. Josh states that:

in everything, God is with us and it just transforms the way that we view our disabilities, the way that we view our situation, and we see God as our provider and our sustainer.

Such assurance is momentous considering the uncertainty that young people living with LL/LTIs face in their lives, but Josh and Helen are quick to assert that their Faith is 'more than ... a coping mechanism'. They describe how prayer is 'a big tool [they use], we always felt better after praying, even if it's been a really hard prayer session'. It also provides an avenue to deal with their situations head on and also the often very difficult emotions that accompany these. Helen says 'sometimes we say that we're very angry ... or sometimes my prayer sessions involve a lot of tears ... we always feel better after talking to God'.

They go on to describe their current situation where one of them is hospitalised and unsure of the future while the other is left to cope alone. Helen says:

sometimes these last few weeks, you know, I've cried and I've said, like, I feel like I'm stuck in a hole and I feel like there's no hope. The truth is, like when I really think about it, I do have hope. Because even in death there is hope, and you know that's a reassuring place to be. And I know that God's got a plan in my life, so you know whatever happens there's hope. ... And God can work good out of any situation, and I've seen him do it time and time again.

The impact of Faith on living with an LL/LTI is clear to see; it can help young people to reframe their lives, perspective and ultimately may help them consider an inevitable aspect of their condition; the prospect of death. In the Living Life to the Fullest Project, we have seen the impact of living with the knowledge that life might be limited or threatened and how this affects so many decisions that disabled young people make in the present (see Chapter 9): whether to enter relationships, take risks and have families as well as how this impacts on their emotional wellbeing.

For me, further fruit has been borne from this complete reshaping of my life; I met my husband, Ed. This union has come from both of us being totally vulnerable with each other and being courageous enough to open up about our individual weaknesses. It was the powerful mix of Faith and disability that led me to the stage where I was able to be vulnerable and I was able to lay my difficulties on the line. As I revealed my frailty and my brokenness to

Ed, I told my journey of surrender. In turn, he exposed his own vulnerability by telling his tale of giving himself up to God. The power in that story was what ultimately won me over.

Ethan and Ed's unconditional love forced me to be faced with an unbalanced mirror in which the reflection of myself was still of someone who was worthless. My sense of self-worth had very much been shaped by my experiences of being in hospital, in positions of extreme vulnerability and dealing with chronic illness as well as carrying the stigma of being a disabled young woman. I found it very hard to see myself as anything but a burden. I had desperately low self-esteem, fostered by the punitive treatment and disbelief I had received in hospital. Yet, even then, I was aware that those views were not the way God saw me and it was this belief in, and relationship with, a God who valued me and thought of me as precious that allowed me to start accepting myself as I am. Everywhere I looked, it seemed that God was reaching out to show me my value. Through the unconditional love of those around me he was showing me my worth and not in spite of my disability, not because of my suffering, but because He has always valued me, even when I was unaware of it. Jeremiah 31: 3 says 'The Lord appeared to us ... saying: "I have loved you with an everlasting love; I have continued to show you My constant love"' and Psalm 37:23 states that God 'delights in every detail of [your] life'.

Becky is also convinced of God's unconditional love: 'I know God loves me and my disability isn't a barrier or a punishment'. She believes she has been made in 'God's image' and explains:

> *I do not believe this is about how our bodies look or work or what we can physically do. I believe it means we are reflections of God's character and his love. Disabled people are made in God's image too, just like non-disabled people. So we are not inferior if our bodies or minds work differently to others.*

I believe God is so much bigger than the things the world deems as limitations and He has an all-encompassing love that lifts me up in a world that typically oppresses. Richard Rohr (2016, n.p.; emphasis added) argues:

> *All are beloved. Everyone – Catholic and Protestant, Christian and Muslim, black and white, gay and straight, able-bodied and disabled, male and female, Republican and Democrat – all are children of God.* We are all members of the Body of Christ, made in God's image, indwelled by the Holy Spirit, whether or not we are aware of this gift.

CONCLUSION

In this chapter, we have acknowledged the complexity of discussing disability and religion but we write in the hope that we can open up a space to honour the lived experiences of disabled young people who have Faith and suggest that perhaps a belief in a suffering God, who embraces the weak and marginalised, can sit with a critical disability studies approach. We recognise the limitations of a chapter that focusses only on Christianity but we hope this chapter might encourage others of different Faiths, and perhaps none, to have conversations about disability, illness and belief.

In what follows we consider three potential points of (inter)connection: humanity; vulnerability and interdependency; and hope.

First, some *thoughts about humanity*. A clear point of connection between critical disability studies and theological debates is the question of what it means to be human. For example, philosopher Eva Feder Kittay's (2019) lived experience of mothering a daughter, who she describes as having 'profound cognitive impairments', has inspired her to reconsider what it means to be human beyond the bounded, rational, individual that has come to signify the human in the tradition of analytic philosophy. Critical disability academics have also asked what it means to be human in the twenty-first century and how disability might enhance these meanings by taking up the work of Rosi Braidotti (Goodley et al., 2014b). Braidotti (2013) pays attention to the role of religion in her seminal text *The Posthuman*. Braidotti is troubled by the turn to secularism in Europe; she argues that this has caused a polarisation of religion and citizenship. Faith has, then, been pushed into the realm of unreason rather than rational judgement, along with passions and emotions (Braidotti, 2013). Braidotti (2013) argues that women, in particular, have suffered from a turn to rational citizenship and politics that excludes passion, emotion *and faith*.

The (inter)connections between critical disability studies scholarship's engagement with the human inevitably intersect with discussions of human vulnerability. Our second point of connection *is the need for an analysis of interdependency and vulnerability*. As we saw, Braidotti (2013, p. 37) seeks to move beyond what she describes as 'lethal binaries' to find different ways of thinking about the human subject as relational and interdependent. This echoes the biblical character Paul who states (over 100 times in the Bible) we are all equally 'en Cristo' or 'in Christ' and He in us. As Richard Rohr (2019, n.p.) explains: 'This identity means humanity has never been separate from God [nor from each other by consequence] – unless and except by its own negative choice'. Goodley et al. (2014b) argue that this posthuman approach fits with the tenets of critical disability studies, but we can also see that it fits with the tenets of Christianity.

Indeed theologians have called for an end to a theology premised on the bifurcation of us and them by 'thinking theologically about ourselves in ways that eliminate the distinction between people with and without disabilities' (Reinders, 2012, p. 35). And, critical disability studies scholarship has also troubled the politics of 'us' and 'them' (Overboe, 1999; Runswick-Cole, 2014). However, the call for a dismantling of 'us' and 'them' has been resisted from within disability studies, by those who depend on disability as an identity in their theoretical engagement and campaigns for social justice (see: Oliver, 1990; Shakespeare, 2006, Vehmas and Watson, 2014). The potential disappearance of disability is always a double-edged sword, especially in a neoliberal welfare state that depends on certainty about disability to sort 'us' from 'them' and in order to redistribute resources to the deserving poor (Ramilow, 2006). We know that disabled people are differentially precarious in austere times (Bates et al., 2017). We have to accept the need to invoke sameness and difference at the same time in order to pursue disability social justice (Goodley and Runswick-Cole, 2014).

Our third point of connection *is the need for Faith*. As we have seen, we live in complex times where disabled people and others routinely experience marginalisation and exclusion. Much of our work has been to expose, to document and to challenge the mundane disablism and ableism that denies disabled people full access to the category of human (Goodley and Runswick-Cole, 2014; Goodley et al., 2014b). Despite or perhaps because of this, we need, and indeed we have, faith in a better future. We have seen acts of resistance and collective activism based on what we have described elsewhere as the disability commons (Runswick-Cole and Goodley, 2017). People have come together to assert their common humanity and to refuse the sorting of 'us' and 'them', worthy and undeserving, human and yet not quite. For examples of such collective activism, we would urge you to follow the social media campaigns: #JusticeforLB and #RightfulLives. Similarly, we eliminate this 'sorting into us and them' when we receive our value from God.

Disabled people are still sometimes viewed as having been punished for some form of wrongdoing, while on the other hand, disability has also been positioned problematically as evidence not of God's anger, but of his benevolence; disability has been described a gift that made disabled people special in God's eyes (Reinders, 2012). Reinders (2012) identifies similar descriptions of disabled people within Jewish and Islamic traditions. Claassens (2012, p. 55) reminds us that:

[i]n Deuteronomy 28:28-9 it is said that God will punish the transgressor with madness and confusion of mind so that he/she will be like a blind person in the dark.

She describes this as one of numerous texts in the Hebrew Bible that view disability as a punishment of God. However, acknowledging this problem does not, of necessity, mean that disabled people should turn away from religion(s). Claassens (2012) offers an alternative response as she calls for biblical texts to be revisited, drawing on a 'hermeneutics of disability' (Reynolds, 2008). A hermeneutics of disability seeks to amplify counter narratives of disability within the Bible. After all, Chataika (2012, p. 125) tells us that the Bible is clear that we are all made in the image of God, and that:

[...] disabled people are not a distortion or an inferior image of God. Their impairments are part of their human identity. Hence, none of us is a surprise, accident or a mistake, and certainly not an embarrassment to God.

Christianity has the potential to offer many people the hope of heavenly solidarity and renewal (Koopman, 2012). This hope is open to all. We end this important chapter with the words of Swartz (2012, p. 90):

[...] faith (and this was not a faith consumed in an authoritarian way, but a faith struggled with by people who had experienced religious exclusion) may be part of what sustains people, and provides a safe and nurturing environment for people whose lives are far more precarious than mine ....

6

RETHINKING SEXUALITY, OUR INTIMATE SELVES AND OUR RELATIONSHIPS WITH OTHERS

KATY EVANS, SALLY WHITNEY-MITCHELL AND KIRSTY LIDDIARD

ACCESSIBLE SUMMARY

- In this chapter, we share what disabled young people said about their sexuality and intimate relationships.

- Young people said they experienced barriers in their sexual and intimate lives.

- Young people talked about others' perceptions, exclusion, digital spaces; personal assistance (PAs) and their intimate and reproductive futures.

INTRODUCTION

Disabled people are routinely excluded from sexual and intimate life (Liddiard, 2018a). They often face a multitude of barriers, including accessing sex education (see Thompson et al., 2001); forming partnerships with others; exclusion from the sexual and social spaces where we might meet partners, such as bars, clubs and pubs; and are regularly subjected to ableist assumptions. Such ableist assumptions often posit disabled people as sexless, sexually inadequate, sexually innocent and/or at risk, or paradoxically, as objects of fetish (Liddiard, 2018a). Much of this is because of the engrained ways in which 'sex' and 'sexuality' come into being in cultures of ableism – the standards of perfection, functionality and ability that dominate our social and cultural worlds (see Goodley, 2014). Liddiard (2018a, p. 2) suggests that 'disability and impairment trouble that which we have come to understand as "(hetero)sex": a naturalised mode of gendered sexual practices that privilege physicality, penetration, form and function'. The material body required for such practices is the normative, controlled and bound body and rational, sane and coherent mind, which many disabled people don't occupy. As a result, disabled people are often denied intimate citizenship (Plummer, 2003), which refers to the rights of people to choose how they organise their personal lives and claim sexual and other intimate identities (see also De Graeve, 2010).

Perhaps not surprisingly, then, sex and sexuality were topics that regularly emerged in disabled young people's stories. Young people we interviewed largely identified as heterosexual, although one participant identified as gay and another as trans. Young people used the interview space to make claims for a sexual and intimate self; to talk freely about their experiences of dating, love, exclusion, care and family-building, and also the ways in which they are routinely subjected to the misconceptions of others, including friends and family. Young people also told us that these forms of exclusion routinely inhibited even the chance to meet friends and build friendships and social networks. At the same time, many participants had low confidence, low sexual self-esteem – particularly young women – and this came through in their narratives explicitly. In this chapter, we share young people's sexual stories.

We begin by outlining what young people told us they found confining about others' perceptions – the multifarious impacts of the widespread disablist and ableist assumptions about disabled people's rights and access to sexuality and intimacy. We then move on to consider what disabled young people told us about exclusion, loneliness and being othered. Later, we explore sexuality and intimacy in relation to young people's digital worlds, considering social media representations of disability, online dating and the problematics and politics of disclosing disability and impairment in digital intimacies with others. We then explore the potentials and perils of PAs and care within sex and relationships. Finally, we end on disabled young people's thoughts on their intimate futures and family-making and building; and it is here that impacts of the nature of their impairments – life-limiting and life-threatening conditions – come into view most clearly. We conclude this chapter by reifying the importance of hearing disabled young people's sexual stories and of listening to and responding to their calls for intimate citizenship (Plummer, 2003).

THE POWER OF OTHERS' ABLEIST PERCEPTIONS

The formation of identity is an important right of passage for all young people but for disabled young people there can be extra challenges to negotiate both internally and externally, especially when this comes to sexual and gender identity (Shakespeare et al., 1996). Most of the participants we spoke to felt they had a strong sense of disability identity which had grown over time, particularly as they entered adulthood. As Christie explains:

I used to think that my disability didn't define me because I think I got sucked into believing that from others. But my disability does define me and it's a big part of my life.

Christie highlights how other people's perceptions can influence how we think about ourselves. This was a common theme when it came to participants seeing themselves as sexual beings. Many welcomed the opportunity to discuss their sexual identity in the interview, which is something that is often routinely denied for disabled young people due to assumptions which (often wrongly) posit them as less interested in sex or lacking desire (Liddiard, 2018a). For example, Christie went on to say: 'Yes, I definitely see myself as a sexual being. I have the same feelings, needs and desires as able-bodied people regardless of my disability'. However, others struggled to see themselves in this way. Anna stated: 'I am not a sexual being! I have never had sex, nor do I desire to do so ever!' There are multiple factors that could influence Anna to reject a sexual identity in such a forthright way – including poor media representations of disability, a lack of positive and relateable role models, internalised ableism over what is classed as 'sex' and 'sexiness' and the normalised inaccessiblity of sexual spaces. We explore some of these factors in this section.

In fact, many felt that others, and societal perceptions in general, did not *see* them as sexual beings which then made it harder for young people to see themselves as such. As Olivia explains:

I think it simply doesn't occur to people. We are almost the invisible section of society. People look but don't see. If they are not personally affected by disability, they don't think about it. I also think we are looked at as children.

Olivia's words express the ways in which disabled people are often readily infantilised, or considered eternal children, particularly people with the label of learning disability, who are routinely denied agency, autonomy and intimate citizenship – our rights and access to intimacy (Ignagni et al., 2016; Liddiard, 2018a). For those with physical impairments who require particular forms of personal care, the need to be physically cared for is also synonymous with childhood (Liddiard and Slater, 2017), which for Olivia exacerbates her feelings of desexualisation.

However, some participants found validation through their partners, as Josh describes:

> *Meeting Helen [partner] and having someone that loves me for me, warts and all, has just helped me accept who I am more and accept the impact that my disability has on my physical appearance and my physical abilities.*

As Josh alludes, body image also played a part in how disabled young people viewed themselves and to what extent they felt able to claim a sexual identity and self (see Abbott et al., 2019). Disability is largely a minority experience which can make it challenging to accept a body that strays from conventional norms as many disabled people are not exposed to images that reflect their appearance as they grow up. In addition, disabled childhoods are often dominated by the medical model; a continuum of appointments, interventions and treatments to get their bodies to perform as optimally as possible (see Runswick-Cole et al., 2018). Seldom is time given to consider the consequences of this drive for normalcy on the individual, no matter how well meaning the intention. Consequently, many participants expressed that aspects of their impairments routinely affected their body image. Anna described using a cape to hide her body:

> *I feel I need to hide my arms or body. I feel safer under it, and have more confidence with it on. To provide some sort of barrier or even armour. Even when it might appear to be far too hot to have it on. Almost as though that cape protects my pink bits, my very insides!...I'm also rather self-conscious that I have to wear incontinence pads of necessity for toileting purposes when I go out. Perhaps wearing the cape is also trying to cover this up for outward appearances.*

Anna's words demarcate the ways in which, as Wilkerson (2002, p. 46) suggests, 'heterosexual women are made, and make themselves, complicit in hierarchies that systematically disadvantage them'. Past this, Anna's testimony above shows the ways in which the intersections of sexism and ableism can subsist starkly for disabled women in relation to body confidence and sexual self-esteem (Liddiard, 2014a). For Catherine, body image insecurities caused her to fear whether she would meet a partner:

I would like to think that I was attractive but the fact is no I don't think so, I don't think the opposite sex find me attractive, I don't think society do either.

It is clear that Catherine has internalised messages about the exceptional standards of beauty in society routinely imposed upon women and feels this does not apply to her as a disabled woman and so therefore her assumption is that no one will be attracted to her.

It is noteworthy that those reporting the greatest difficulties with body image were women, which fits with the broader fascination with women's aesthetic bodies in wider society (see Bartky, 1990). In addition to the societal expectations placed on all women, disabled women occupy bodies and minds that may stray from the idealised notions of beauty and therefore can face more difficulty accepting their bodies in a culture which strives for perfection (see Liddiard, 2014a, 2018a). These self-perceptions, often shaped as much by sexism as ableism, represent one of the several factors that disabled young people have to negotiate when it comes to forming relationships with others, both platonic and sexual. Another of the factors that can exacerbate this is difficulties around socialising and integration, which is where we now turn.

LONELINESS, DIFFICULTIES IN SOCIALISING AND FEELING OTHERED

Accessing social spaces and feeling included is a challenge that many disabled young people regularly face. They are often seen as the 'other' and, as we have highlighted in other chapters of the book, the onus is often on the disabled person to undertake various forms of emotional work and labour to counteract, or live with, these messages. As a result, some participants reported feeling lonely and felt disability set them apart from their peers for a variety of physical and psychosocial reasons, which then made physical barriers feel more intense and isolating. Jane explains:

For me it's not that easy to just 'grab a drink after work' – because I have to think about my own fatigue, I have to think about what train I am able to get back to where I live, my carer hours and things like that. Going out and socialising isn't as easy for me, it is going to be a longer process to make friends with people.

Catherine feels that physical barriers have inhibited her from making friends:

Being in a wheelchair poses the obvious problem of not being
able to go to places that don't have wheelchair access so people's
houses, even today I can't go to anybody's houses, if they have
got a small step I can take my ramps but in general I never go to
people's houses because it is too much trouble, so no you can't
really go to any house parties, you can't really go to people's
birthday parties.

Here, the onus is on Catherine to do the work in order to be socially
included and she highlights the 'trouble' she feels it is and the (often visible)
labour of being included. Disability can present a conundrum where a person
is simultaneously highly visible and invisible. Lack of awareness of problems
around accessibility and *fears* of the marked lack of access can lead to disabled people being further isolated. We see this in Jane's words:

very few people on the [university] course would have been exposed
to disability before and so they didn't ever approach me and I felt
like they just had no idea how to talk to me so therefore they didn't
even try.

Similarly, Sam fears the labour involved with accommodating their disability actually increases their isolation:

I worry that I'll be lonely for a long time. That people will always
find disability and the accommodations I need to be difficult and
make me not worth bothering with.

Anna went on to say:

It's always been difficult to make friends, because of the barrier that
my disability creates between myself and others. And when you
reach eighteen, there is very little in the way of organised clubs, and
chances to meet other people anymore.

Some participants felt that media portrayals of disability and disabled people's lives fuelled misconceptions of and misinformation about disability, and
that this also could make the formation of relationships all the more difficult.
Sam commented, 'there's the ever present theme of "I'd rather be dead than
disabled" like in the film *Me Before You*'. *Me Before You* (2016) is posited as
a love story in which the disabled male protagonist chooses death over life
on the basis that he doesn't want to live a disabled life; he also chooses death
over 'inflicting' disability on the woman he loves. Some participants worried
that such dominant narratives of disability and intimacy – *Me Before You*

grossed $208 million at the box office in 2016 – impacted non-disabled people's understandings of disability. Others commented that it pushed unhelpful ableist assumptions that death is preferable, and that disability is incompatible with love and intimacy to the foreground. Such narratives also propagate the idea that disability, intimacy and love are either inherently traumatic or troublesome or will have a tragic end. Such ableist imagery makes relating to disability on any other level but one of tragedy challenging, and can also be a reflection of non-disabled people's fears about the fragility of life, the body and mortality (see Chapter 9).

Media portrayals often present a person's illness or impairment as being the key source of their difficulties and a cause for pity (Barnes, 1992; Liddiard, 2014a), which Anna argues is inaccurate: 'It's not really the having to cope with the physical condition of cerebral palsy, but much more the having to deal with the stigma created by society'. Jane further reflects that the way disability is presented in the media fails to realistically represent the roundness and vibrancy of disabled people's lives and the ability to have meaningful relationships. She said:

> I think it's not necessarily the messages that I have received so
> much as ones that I haven't, like I haven't seen a disabled woman
> on TV who just has a normal relationship and her disability isn't
> a huge part of that storyline … it is always the disability is more
> important than the emotional connection between the two people.

It is not surprising, then, that disabled young people reported that the representation of sexual relationships and disability in dominant media spaces subsist in a problematic binary whereby disability is either misconstrued and misunderstood, or conspicuously absent and invisible. The young people we spoke to were understandably concerned about how these disability discourses could impact upon finding a partner.

INTIMATE SELVES AND DIGITAL LIVES

At many points in this book, we have highlighted the positives of digital space. However, when it came to social inclusion and loneliness this was a double-edged sword for many disabled young people in our project. Social media is undoubtedly a form of human connection for many, but it is also a highly individualistic and aspirational space where many people present their 'best lives' over reality, which many young people in our project said was confining. As Olivia explained:

*For me it [social media] is a lifeline! Without it, I would feel
INCREDIBLY lonely & depressed. I mostly use Facebook
Messenger in order to stay in touch with friends & to meet others
in a similar position to myself.*

However, Jude felt seeing people's lives displayed on social media increased
her feelings of loneliness:

*I can see things on social media and see people living their lives,
continuing on, and I am not or I am not living it to how I would
want to be living it to, it goes back to aspirations – I want to be
doing more but I can't and that is difficult to swallow.*

Social media can also be a space where inspiration porn around disability
reigns supreme (Liddiard, 2014a). Liddiard (2014a, p. 94) states that:

*the terms 'inspiration porn' and 'cripspiration' refer to typically
ableist images of disability which represent either a person with
disability as 'inspiring' (usually doing an everyday activity, rather
than anything actually heroic or inspiring) or which rely upon
disability in order to inspire or otherwise shape the behaviours and/
or attitudes of the audience or viewer.*

Thus, social media can denote for disabled young people yet another social
space where disabled personhood is restricted and reduced to one dimension
(Liddiard, 2014a). Young people in our project were highly conscious of such
portrayals of disability and how it impacted their use of social media. Many
expressed feeling frustrated when others infantilised them or viewed them
through a lens of 'inspiration' rather than seeing their ordinary human experiences. Our participants reported how such imagery can be both confining and
deeply reductionist for disabled young people. This discrepancy between reality and how disability and youth are perceived by others created more barriers
to being socially accepted; as Rachel explains: 'I think my flatmates expected
me to be in bed at 9 and it was breaking news if I swore or drank alcohol
for the first few weeks'. In this section of the chapter, we consider the role of
digital space in disabled young people's experiences of sexuality and intimacy.

Disability and Disclosure in Online Dating

In this chapter, so far disabled young people have articulated their experiences of exclusion in their material and social worlds. Disabled young people
described to us the multiple barriers they have to overcome when finding and

meeting partners, such as difficulties with access in social spaces, the general misconceptions of disability in society and potential partners' expectations and (mis)understandings of disability. If this was the case with everyday inter-actions, the challenges were seemingly multiplied when negotiating the world of dating, particularly in the realm of digital space. Many disabled young people told us that online dating can be extremely difficult and incredibly intimidating. This is in addition to the increased vulnerability it can take for disabled people to show their bodies and selves online and the often perilous disclosures they can feel forced to make in order to secure a date and/or con-nection. For some participants, the process of online dating caused them to question their own self-worth and disabled identity. Even those participants who spoke of positive and prideful disabled identities spoke of the intense shame that can materialise through the politics of disclosure during digital introductions and intimate interactions. In this section, we intersplice Co-researcher Sally's reflections with participants' experiences of looking for and finding partners online.

Notably, difficulties experienced in young people's physical and social worlds in no way reduced the desire to have relationships. Co-researcher Sally comments that, for anyone, finding a partner is not always easy, and that she, just like many other disabled young people, has to think creatively about how to meet people and consider the boundaries of disability disclosure and other personal details such as the ability to have families. As Sally reflects:

> I am a young woman, full time wheelchair user who is chronically and severely ill. How can I have encounters in romantic locations if I can't get to them? But these hurdles don't affect my desire to find a partner. And if I'm not able to go 'out' to find them, I'll have to get them to come to me. As has been the way for me for a long time, the internet has been my way of bringing things into my bubble from the outside world: My groceries, the clothing, friends (albeit in virtual spaces).

As Sally's words show, a key theme in disabled young people's online experiences when it comes to dating is the *disclosure* of disability. Even the language of 'disclosure' denotes that disability can subsist as a secret to be revealed. However, such a 'reveal' comes with a raft of difficulties, such as how much to be open about disability on one's profile, as Sally shares:

> I set about writing a profile that really reflected who I am as a person. The things that make me tick, the things that I care about and what I enjoy about my life. Basically, I wanted to clearly convey ME, but how much of who I am is that I'm a disabled woman?

Our disabled young participants struggled with disclosure, too. As Sam recalls, 'Oh it's a nightmare! ... I never know what time I should tell people that I'm chronically ill and mobility impaired. It's a delicate balance'. Timing and how much one needs to disclose is a real difficulty; as Rachel affirms, 'I found it hard to know how to, when or if I even needed to let men know I was disabled'.

For those with visible impairments, sometimes the timing of disclosure seems inevitable as their impairments may be apparent in profile pictures. Yet, this isn't always the case and once again there were questions around what to present and whether visible disability pushes away potential partners. As Ella notes, '... whether it be hooking up in real life or online dating you say the word wheelchair and people run for the hills'. Co-researcher Sally struggled with the same issue:

> *Obviously, everyone aims to present their best side so I wasn't going to post any pics in intensive care, but what should I post? I am someone who can look quite healthy when feeling good and sat on an ordinary chair, but was that an accurate representation? I decided that actively drawing attention to my health problems wasn't the way to attract people ....*

Yet, for some, it's more clear-cut, as Ramesh describes:

> *[...] it is clear in my pictures that I use a wheelchair. I think that is the best way, if the wheelchair bothers them then they are not the right person.*

But for others, it led to doubts around constructed disabled identities and selfhood, as Sally describes:

> *I had never questioned myself so much. Was I as honest a person as I thought or was I entering into some kind of deception by not labelling my photos, 'Caution: disabled woman!'? This begs the question; how much of my identity is private and how much is public? Because I'm disabled, is the public somehow more entitled to know more about me and in doing so does my identity become publicly owned?*

Sally's words above reveal the double-bind of disclosure in online dating: the fact that in ableist cultures disability is often cast as the main identity or characteristic for disabled people – disability serves as a primary public identity. The double-bind comes, then, when disability *isn't* the first thing a person wants to affirm about themselves, and thus 'not revealing' is reduced to some kind of falsehood or secrecy.

For many, a key factor underpinning the difficulties surrounding dating and disclosure is based on the belief that non-disabled people are less likely to want to date a disabled person. There are a whole host of reasons why disabled young people feel this way; as Rachel states, 'I think you're viewed less as a potential date because of the assumption we're asexual'. While Jude believes that disability is a misunderstood and a taboo subject:

> [...] people generally don't see themselves with someone who is disabled because of the way disability is perceived. It is normally seen more that you would be with someone and then they would become disabled, not that you get with someone who is disabled ... when (actually) it happens quite a lot.

Perhaps most devastatingly, Olivia describes below why she believes non-disabled people don't want to date disabled people. Her words represent the intensity of psycho-emotional disablism – what Thomas (1999, p. 60) calls 'the socially engendered undermining of emotional well-being' – which Liddiard (2014a) states can exacerbate the cultural and political denial of a sexual and intimate self. As Reeve (2012, p. 24) articulates, 'psycho-emotional disablism operates at the private level, restricting who people can be'. It encompasses 'having to deal with hurtful comments, stigmatising actions of others and internalised oppression which can undermine someone's psycho-emotional wellbeing and sense of self' (Reeve, 2012, p. 24). Olivia said:

> I can't see how or why anyone would look at me & want to date me. I don't feel I have anything to offer. It sounds awful, but I think if I were able-bodied, it's highly unlikely that I would ever consider dating a disabled person versus an able-bodied person. Therefore, I have no expectations.

Yet, some disabled young people chose to specifically date other disabled people, with the belief that doing so was somehow 'safer' in that the disabled potential partner also had an understanding of disability. As Rachel states:

> [...] depending on their impairment, I felt physically equal or more able than the disabled men I've dated so felt safe and in control ... . Whereas I fear a non-disabled man would be more able to take advantage of me.

We can see here the inherent problematic assumptions that disabled men can never be exploitative and/or violent (see Liddiard, 2014a).

Co-researcher Sally noted that, having got past what she called 'the mine-field that is what to put in a profile', interactions with dates (often via messaging) begin, which typically throws up similar problems around managing disability information and experience. Sally said:

> [...] disclosure reared its ugly head again. I started to get suspicious
> – no one seemed to mention my health or question my wheelchair
> in their messages. I considered that perhaps they were waiting for
> a bit of back and forth banter before coming out with it, and some
> did. However, on the whole I wasn't questioned and I soon started
> to feel deceitful. I asked myself why? Should the state of my body
> functioning be public knowledge? Would I expect someone else
> to immediately tell me about their bowel habits? Does my visible
> disability entitle others to probe? As I was chatting to guys, I began
> to casually ask if they had spotted my wheelchair. Once that had
> been pointed out, I felt 'duty-bound' to mention my illness. Once
> again I asked myself why? Am I public property because my body is
> different from the norm? Previously, when I wasn't in a wheelchair
> but still severely unwell (so not visibly disabled), was my body
> owned less by the general public? I know for certain that I felt less
> pressure to explain myself immediately. But how much should I
> reveal? And why did I have an uncomfortable feeling of stripping
> myself bare to strangers on the internet when I started to tell them
> about my health?

Sally's words reiterate the complex negotiation that often can happen around privacy, (others') curiosity and the visual context of digital spaces for disabled young people. Choosing what to tell, and when, and to whom, and why, was reported by many participants to be incredibly difficult, as this section has shown. Thus, just because digital spaces can be far more physically accessible (for some), this doesn't necessarily mean the usual barriers and forms of work required of disabled young people in intimate life are absent. In the next section, we explore the relationships between care, support and sexual and intimate identities.

MEDIATING LOVE, SEX AND CARE

After articulating the many challenges in meeting, connecting and finding a suitable partner with whom to have a relationship, disabled young people often described the difficulties associated with being in loving and sexual relationships as recipients of care and support. For example, Jane said that 'there is the awkwardness of dating when you have a carer with you all the time'. Ella spoke of the toll having care has placed on her relationship: 'my relationship is strained with my partner of 6 years because of the invasion of in-home help several times a day'. Her choice of the word 'invasion' here demarcates her experiences of care and intimacy as burdensome. In this section, we explore experiences of care as an integral part of love and intimacy. The words we share below echo participants' realities of having 24 hour care from PAs:

I have 24/7 care. That means I have a carer with me at all times. That's not sexy! How can I anticipate private, intimate moments with someone special if I've always got an entourage? After all, going on first dates and feeding back how it went to someone else can be fun, but living in very close confines with a carer (who is paid to check in on you and your wellbeing) is entirely different. From the embarrassment of having a carer ask where to store the contraception being unpacked from a grocery delivery, to the harsh reality of having to keep sexual encounters quiet and discreet, the awkwardness seems unavoidable. It shouldn't be the case that I feel I have to keep noise to a minimum and my partner can't make a hygiene trip to the bathroom without getting re-dressed, but these are the types of accommodations we make. Having someone constantly present in the house means we can't have spontaneous intimate encounters in any room in the house and that, even when in the bedroom, the inevitably of a carer knocking on the door with medication or medical intervention means that even these are rushed and planned a while before hand in coded whispers. How much this has affected our relationship I can't tell. All I know is that he is incredibly patient with the whole situation and the fact that his home feels more like a medical clinic than a honeymoon!

The words above show the emotional labours involved in managing sexuality and desire in the context of care, assistance and support. The calls for privacy here are marked – having to be discreet (in her own home), to hide, rush and talk in 'coded whispers' all speak to the reality that, for some, the disabled body is always on display and subject to (caring) others (Taleporos and McCabe, 2001; Earle, 1999). Ensuring privacy, for yourself and often also for your partner, was a key priority for our disabled young participants in intimate relationships with others.

However, Helen and Josh – one of the only couples we interviewed – describe the difficulty in meeting each other's sexual needs when both have physical impairments, and where one of the couple is living with a progressive impairment. They share particular concern about how impairment progression might impact their future sex life and their need for PA input:

> Helen: I often can't do what Josh wants me to do because I get tired or I can't reach and it's difficult because my condition is progressive, we know over time our sex life is going to change and that comes with anxiety ....

Despite the fact that they are aware of the likely future need for greater levels of PA support and have discussions around this, it doesn't alleviate the desire to share sexual intimacy with as little input from others as possible:

> Helen: At the moment, our input from PAs is very remote. We might get them to put us in to a certain position or and then leave us and then, unless we drop something on the floor that we really need, we don't really like get them involved at all and we don't really want them to be any more involved than that, but what happens as time goes on?

It is clear to see that what Helen and Josh desire – to be independent during intimacy – is discordant with their physical needs. As Sakellariou (2006, p. 104) suggests, while any couple may face difficulties with sex, 'when one or both of the partners are disabled somehow an utterly private issue is transformed into a public one'. The contemplation of a future increase in support leads to frustration and worry. And yet, this couple is clear on how to manage these difficulties as best they can. They also demonstrate how disabled people often develop strategies in intimate relationships with others – for example, openness and communication in their intimacy – that may benefit how *all* people negotiate and experience intimacy, as well as other disabled young people. They state:

> Helen: I think it comes down to communication again and this is what we talk about when we do talks; the importance of communicating continuously in your sex life. The most important conversation we have is about sexual frustration and managing that and [that] sex has to be fun.

This difficulty was further, and perhaps more keenly, highlighted by disabled young people who had family members amongst their carers. Hunter said:

[...] there are obviously questions of what it means to be gay, what the gay lifestyle is... you probably couldn't live that kind of lifestyle all the time ... I am quite reliant on family as well so that probably makes it quite awkward ... you know people are aware of it but it's not something you probably want to discuss with a parent you know whether you are gay or straight to be honest but it just adds another layer of complexity or awkwardness really.

Hunter's experiences here show the 'extra' difficulties that can come with being an LGBT+ disabled young person (see Abbott and Howarth, 2007; Dinwoodie et al., 2020). Quite often the presence of care was something young people had to get used to, particularly in the context of their sexual and intimate lives. As Sam said:

[...] yes it was definitely emotionally challenging at first, having someone in my house every day and helping me with some intimate parts of life, but it's a bit easier now.

Co-researcher Ruth suggested that the ways in which PAs and carers viewed her could have an impact on the extent to which she could ask for support around intimacy:

Perhaps carers responsible solely for my personal care view me less as a person and individual, focussing on sorting out things like washing and toileting and transferring and so on. Things like personal privacy come into this, and perhaps seeing me as a whole individual becomes slightly obscured by this whole mechanical process.

Ruth's words above reiterate the ways in which she may be reduced to a series of tasks, rather than a person with particular care and support needs. Her whole self would be inclusive of her intimate self, which is something she doesn't yet feel able to approach as part of her care requirements.

This section has shown the complexities that subsist between having a body that requires particular forms of care, privacy, and the expression of an intimate and sexual self. Many participants said that they lacked privacy generally, and that this was exacerbated through caring arrangements, and particularly familial caring. Therefore, access to privacy and support – or rather a lack of it – could be a significant factor in shaping young people's sexual selves and their sexual expression. Next, we turn to participants' perspectives on their sexual, intimate and reproductive futures.

THE ROLE OF EXPECTATION: CONSIDERING OUR SEXUAL, INTIMATE AND REPRODUCTIVE FUTURES

Intimate and reproductive futures were a common theme for participants when discussing sexuality and intimacy. As Sam explained:

> *I do have faith. I have many friends with the same conditions as me who are married or engaged or in a loving relationship. I know it's not impossible – just difficult.*

Despite this, young people were clear to us of the low expectations for their intimate lives and relationships, which were said to be both imposed by society and close others, such as parents, family and friends. Often this extended to their futures: the expectation to have a long term partner, marry and have a family of their own. Participants readily talked about the ways in which their intimate futures were routinely cast into doubt, because of misinformed assumptions about disability and sex/uality. In this final section, we discuss the nature of life-limiting and life-threatening impairment (LL/LTI) – the suggestion of short/er lives and lifespans – and the impacts these realities can have on the sexual and intimate lives of disabled young people.

The potential for a shorter than average lifespan was an important consideration for some young people we interviewed; even where young people felt it didn't make a difference to their future planning around relationships and family-building, often the views of families got in the way. For example, one participant recalled an experience whereby a family member had sought to 'warn' their partner as to the 'implications' of having a long term disabled partner:

> *When he proposed I was obviously over the moon – I was in love. However, my brother took him to one side and gave him a full interrogation about whether he understood the long term implications of being with me for life. What he might miss out on, what he would have to give up to live with me, etc. This was done with the best of intentions but clearly was distressing to me. However, my fiancé came out of the 'interview' both a little inebriated (to deal with the interrogation) and still dead set on marriage. I couldn't have asked for a better partner.*

Thus, the role and opinions of family can have a huge impact on disabled young people and their partners, often causing them to doubt their ability to have relationships and longer term valued intimacies with others. Reeve (2004, p. 91) suggests that trusted people within disabled people's own social networks, such as family members and friends, are often 'agents of psycho-emotional disablism' and that the emotional suffering that can occur is actually more acute when coming from those with whom a trust (or proximity) is shared (see also Reeve, 2002; Liddiard, 2018a). In her book, Liddiard (2018a, p. 64) argues that this only serves 'to reinforce ableist cultural tropes of disabled sexual selfhood as both inappropriate and improbable' (see also Wilkerson, 2002). When drawing on the possibilities of future lives and expectations around progression of impairment and possible early death, this was markedly exacerbated for disabled young people in our project.

Quite often, such assumptions were internalised by participants; for example, Helen, who was interviewed with her husband Josh, described her own self-doubts prior to meeting him:

> [...] In terms of the way I perceive myself, for a long time, I really didn't think that I was capable of dating because emotionally I didn't think I would be capable of it and then I just thought it wouldn't be fair to get into a relationship with somebody and them spending their whole life with me going in and out of hospital and then maybe dying and leaving them alone.

But once Helen had begun to consider dating, her mother had certain expectations of what her intimate future might look like. Once Helen had overcome her own worries, her family's expectations around her future health began to weigh heavily:

> My parents were still coming to terms with me being disabled and what that meant. My mum especially had a parental dream of what she wanted my future to look like. She wanted a future for me that she now realises is not going to happen. When I eventually did decide to start looking for a partner, I think my mum got excited. She got this idea into her head that this big strapping bloke was going to pick me up out of my wheelchair and do all my personal care. I wasn't going to need carers because he was going to be my full time carer and he was going to rescue me. He was going to have some high powered job and somehow meet all of my financial needs as well. My mum had in her head of how the situation was going to be solved.

We can see that, initially, Helen's mother assumed the end of an intimate future upon the arrival of disability; later her expectations changed to a hyper-masculine non-disabled figure for her daughter. Helen goes on to describe how this expectation that ultimately was different to what actually transpired – Helen met and married a disabled man with physical impairment, Josh – which proved to be a further challenge for her family:

> *Helen: Then I introduced them to Josh by video and annoyingly the first thing my mum said was 'he has got a really strange voice (due to his disability).*

> *Josh: I found it quite a challenge to get Helen's parents to accept me, particularly her mum, because I think there is hope of finding a husband that would whisk her off her feet and rescue her from her disability.*

The perceptions of family hint at the attitudes of society towards disability. We suggest, then, that internalised ableism is not only the preserve of disabled people, but that ableist ideals can inevitably be internalised by family members and close others (Reeve, 2004). As Rachel articulates: 'some of my family have found it difficult to view me as an independent young woman and often unconsciously put limiting beliefs onto me'.

One of the most conflicting self-perceptions we came across during the research was disabled young people rejecting the idea of having intimate relationships with others on the basis that doing so would be unfair – a narrative markedly similar to the plot in the film *Me Before You* (2016), as mentioned earlier in the chapter. The context of LL/LTI inevitably exacerbated such views. For some disabled young people, this made dating seem out of the realms of possibility altogether. As Olivia explains:

> *[...] because I am so aware of the seriousness of my condition & the fact it is life-limiting, I am reluctant to enter into romantic relationships.*

As a result, some disabled young people chose not to date, deeming it the lowest priority for them with the limited lifespan that can come with life-limiting and life-threatening conditions:

> *Ruth: In my view, dating is the least important thing in my life. I know this may seem controversial, but I don't feel like I need the security of an intimate relationship... I know it is important to some disabled people, to validate themselves, but not in my case. I feel that my relationships with friends are more than enough for me, I don't feel the need for a sexual relationship.*

Inevitably, our intimate futures with others, for many, will include having children and/or building family. Olsen and Clarke (2003, p. xi) state that 'parenting is simultaneously one of the most private, intimate roles that we undertake and yet is one subject to the greatest public gaze and scrutiny'. For disabled people, the barriers to becoming parents and accessing rights to raise children can be significant. Disabled parenting is often surveilled, scrutinised and pathologised, readily underpinned by assumptions that disability inevitably has a negative impact on both the child and the family as a whole (Olsen and Clarke, 2003). We see this in Ella's words, where she speaks of the judgements of others:

> *I'm more worried how others perceive me despite being very sure of myself ... I worry people may pity me particularly for my condition and judge me for carrying on with my life, having children knowing it's likely I won't see them get married, have kids, etc.*

Here ambiguity around Ella's lifespan is drawn into her mothering and the care she can give to others. She states she is 'very sure of herself' but that, despite this, she is an object of pity in claiming and enacting her rights to motherhood and family. The assumption that she will die before seeing her children undertake certain normative life stages (getting married, having their own children) takes centre stage, when a long life is not guaranteed for any parent.

Disabled young people in our project routinely carried out forms of emotional work (see Liddiard, 2014a) in negotiating their own feelings about their reproductive futures, but many spoke of *carrying* a feeling of responsibility for their partners' reproductive futures, too. Co-researcher Sally commented that, beyond sexual experiences, she felt questioned even more intensely about her reproductive potential:

> *Yet another hurdle lay ahead, I found myself being asked extremely personal, in depth questions about my health and state of my body. For example, I would be openly asked whether I could have kids, if my conditions were genetic, etc. I realised that although these men weren't looking for a quick hook up, they were looking for so-called 'perfect' wives and mothers. 'I want a woman who will give me a rugger, bugger of a son' one said. It seems that my suitability as a match was entirely defined by my reproductive potential. And considering my body didn't reflect that of an 'able' woman, I didn't qualify.*

Sally's words here echo that of disabled feminist Waxman-Fiduccia (2000, p. 169), who argues that 'sexual rights have always and only been awarded to those who are proclaimed to deliver quality offspring'. Thus, as someone with a life-threatening impairment, who is (incorrectly) deemed to have a compro-mised ability to *produce* healthy children, her sexual and intimate rights and citizenship are curtailed. Many participants in our project spoke of how they were subject to such discourses, and their words often showed the extent to which this had been internalised. Thus, many seldom spoke about future par-enthood and family-building, and where this was referred to it was typically in the realm of LL/LTI being a barrier to building families. This echoes other research that argues parenting and reproductive justice, as a form of intimate citizenship (Plummer, 2003), is routinely denied to disabled people (Olsen and Clarke, 2003; Andrews and Ayers, 2016).

CONCLUSION

The narratives we have explored throughout this chapter reify the impor-tance of sexuality and intimacy for disabled young people living with LL/LTIs. Our participants' experiences reveal that they are routinely denied intimate citizenship (Plummer, 2003) and can face myriad barriers to sexual life and intimate relationships with others, both in the present across material and digital worlds and when planning for the future (see also De Graeve, 2010). Our findings lead us to conclude, then, that sexual and intimate life is a space in adulthood that can consist of tensions, isolation, rejection, disclosure and a significant amount of emotional work and labour to manage and negoti-ate for disabled young people living with LL/LTIs. Despite this, we want to emphasise here that while such challenges are a reality for many, disabled young people can and do have fulfilling sexual lives and meaningful intima-cies with others. Moreover, disability and impairment can also bring positives to sexual and intimate relations with others: increased communication with partners and different forms of sexual exploration to name but a couple that our participants have emphasised in their stories. What our participants have most clearly articulated, then, is the need to *listen* to disabled people's sexual stories; to *consider* their sexual rights and access to intimate citizenship; and ensure that we focus on accessibility within their social and sexual worlds in order to change attitudes and encourage sexual self-esteem and worth.

7

LABOUR IN THE LIVES OF DISABLED YOUNG PEOPLE

KATY EVANS, SALLY WHITNEY-MITCHELL AND
KATHERINE RUNSWICK-COLE

ACCESSIBLE SUMMARY

- In this chapter, we focus on forms of labour and work.
- We show the ways in which disabled young people carry out lots of work across their lives.
- We tell you about the ways we have created an accessible workspace.

INTRODUCTION

The focus of this chapter is labour in the lives of young people living with life limiting and life-threatening impairment (LL/LTIs). We chose the word 'labour' carefully. Too often, the word 'work' is associated with traditional forms of paid labour rather than with the complex forms of labour that take place in our homes and in our relationships with other people. The experiences of young people living with LL/LTIs, as we see below, illuminate the inadequacy of narrow and normative understandings of 'work' and reveal instead the multiplicity and complexities of labour, including emotional labour, in its many forms in a variety of places, spaces and times.

Drawing on critical disability studies, this chapter begins with the assumption that disability's disruptive potential has much to offer understanding and practices in the world of work for everyone (Goodley et al., 2019). Our discussion draws on three theoretical resources which inform critical disability studies: emotional labour (Hochschild, 1983), crip time (Kafer, 2013) and critical geographies of disability and space (Kitchin, 1998).

We explore multiple forms of (emotional) labour enacted in the different spaces across disabled young people's lives. We conclude by reviewing the 'workplace' we created during The Living Life to the Fullest Project by offering some 'crip alternatives' to narrow and normative working practices which can routinely exclude and marginalise disabled people.

THEORETICAL RESOURCES

Our first theoretical resource is the concept of emotional labour (Hochschild, 1983). We have spoken about the importance of recognising emotional labour in the lives of disabled young people elsewhere in this book (see Chapter 4 for a discussion of emotional labour in relation to human–animal relationships and Chapter 9 for a discussion of the emotional labour of experiencing grief and managing wellbeing). Emotional labour refers to the work involved when a person feels that they must hide or change their feelings in order to manage the emotions of others. Crucially, Hochschild's (1983, p. 7) influential text discusses emotional labour in the context of *the paid work* of flight attendants who she observed as being 'nicer than natural' in order to perform their duties. Hochschild (1983, p. 7) explains how service work requires employees to 'induce or suppress feeling in order to sustain the outward countenance that produces the proper state of mind in others'. Emotional labour has since been applied beyond the service industry, particularly in relation to care (e.g. Staden, 1998). Just as Hochschild's (1983) original study focussed on emotional labour on the part of those who delivered services in the hospitality industry. In the context of disability, the focus has often been on the experiences of (paid) carers, rather than the emotional labour of disabled people receiving care, as we noted in Chapter 4. This is problematic as it is based on a mistaken assumption that disabled people are not, themselves, caregivers, when the evidence reveals that many disabled people take on caring roles (see Liddiard, 2014a). Another problem is the narrow focus on the task-based aspects of caregiving, rather than understanding care as a relational activity in which caregiver and recipients of care are both engaged in forms of labour. Here, we foreground the (emotional) labour of those who receive care.

Our second theoretical resource is crip time (Kafer, 2013) (also discussed in Chapter 9, relating to young people's desires). In her discussion of crip time, Kafer (2013) argues that ability, as the desirable normal state/condition of being, permeates our understanding of time (Ljuslinder et al., 2020). In describing crip time, Kafer (2013, p. 27) suggests that 'rather than bend disabled bodies and minds to meet the clock, crip time bends the clock to meet disabled bodies and minds'. We agree with Kafer that disability allows us to think differently about life and to expose and challenge narrow and normative ways of thinking about time.

Our third resource is related to critical geographies of disability and space (Kitchin, 1998). Kitchin (1998) argued that space, as well as time, plays a crucial role in reproducing and sustaining disablist practices. He argues that spaces are organised to keep disabled people 'in their place' but also to construct disabled people as 'out of place' (Kitchin, 1998:, p.343). By paying attention to the spatialities of disability, we can think about the ways in which labour is conceptualised and paid work is accessed as a mechanism for keeping disabled people in their place (as receivers, not givers, of care) and out of place (as members of the workforce).

For us, disability opens up crip alternatives, or different ways of thinking, about seemingly mundane practices, like labour, that are too often shaped by neoliberal assumptions about the human value of 'able' bodies (Goodley et al., 2014b). We are interested in the mundane and emotional labour, including advocacy work, that disabled young people engage with at different times and in different spaces in order to stay alive.

At the same time, we must recognise that disabled young people, like many others, desire paid work. And so, our crip alternative to work is underpinned by two assumptions:

1. Everyone is engaged in labour of some sort, which takes place in different times and spaces and in different forms, all of which should be recognised and have value.

2. Paid work is valued by disabled young people, and there is a need to expand the working practices to ensure that paid work is accessible to all those who desire it.

These assumptions directly contradict traditional approaches which prioritise paid work over all other forms of labour and which focus on the 'rehabilitation' of disabled people in order to prepare them for work (Frank, 2016). We want to shift thinking away from the idea that disabled people must be 'work ready' to ensuring that 'workplaces are ready' for a diverse workforce.

In the first section, Co-researcher Ruth reflects on the everyday work she has to do to keep her body going. Building on this, Co-researcher Sally explores the emotional labour she has endured to be recognised and accepted in two medicalised spaces: the hospital and medical school. In the next section, Co-researchers Sally and Katy write about emotional labour as advocacy work in the context of community and in social care spaces. Accounts are interspersed with reflections from the disabled young participants we spoke to about the (emotional) labour they are engaged with. Finally, we reflect on our own working practices as a project team as we explore crip alternatives to working practices that are framed by normative expectations of work in time and space.

THE LABOUR OF STAYING ALIVE: EMOTIONAL LABOUR AND BODY WORK

In her blog (Spurr, 2019, n.p.), Co-researcher Ruth, reflects on what her life's 'work' has become. She explains the early morning work she does to keep her body going:

> *Every morning I wake up, breathe first of all – that's a good sign – hope I've not been sick on myself overnight, which can happen a lot. Start the morning medication, so multiple tablets to be crushed, dose up 10 to 15 syringes worth of medication to keep my heart, bladder, bowels, immune system and chronic pain in check, and give all these medications through a special tube which sits in my small intestines. And then do all the other morning treatments ... then detach the old feed, re-attach the new feed, flush one of the tubes, empty, wash all the syringes, with help because otherwise I would literally be by the sink the whole day. Have a shower, if I've got the energy. Empty the drainage bags, measure the input, measure the output. Attach new bags. Clean tube sites, change old stoma, put new stoma bag on, make sure that's OK. Other dressings all as needed as dependent.*

Ruth makes visible the day-to-day labour that takes place in her home, just to stay alive, as she documents the everyday practicalities of managing medical technology. Ruth's body cannot bend to the normative expectations of a timely morning routine. Rather than seeing Ruth's morning as out of time, we need to crip these normative expectations of time and value the everyday labour that Ruth engages with to get up in the morning (Kafer, 2013).

In the project, we have found that disabled young people face challenges in their lives which require actions they *have* to take in order to survive, often requiring tremendous resilience, and, crucially, that these actions carry emotional burdens too, which are exacerbated by normative expectations such as how long it 'should' take to get up in the morning. For Co-researcher Sally, there is additional emotional labour necessary to stay alive, which is where we now turn.

EMOTIONAL LABOUR IN MEDICALISED SPACES

There have been so many times when I'm not in my wheelchair or not visibly disabled to on-lookers that I have been asked what I do for 'work'. It seems that in the non-disabled world we live in, the go-to question to introduce oneself or to make small talk is 'what do you do?' For so long, I have rallied against this question but at the same time been unable to provide an 'acceptable answer'. How do I answer such a seemingly innocuous question in a short snappy way that even sketches the outline of the 'work' I do? Nobody seems to understand that what I 'do' in my life, in my every waking moment, is just as (and I would argue far more) exhausting, labour intensive, nerve-racking and critical than any paid job. The labour of trying to stay alive in medicalised spaces can be all consuming but is rarely recognised.

When I first became unwell nobody knew what was wrong with me. I went through years of misdiagnosis, maltreatment and lack of any care provision before it was fully understood what my conditions were and what needed to happen for me to receive any appropriate treatment. There was continuous toil on my part to be recognised as a valued human being with hopes, dreams and aspirations and as an expert in my own life. I recollect a particularly difficult period of my life when I was hospitalised for 7.5 months, where every moment seemed like a fight to be accepted and believed. In hospital, I engaged in the labour of making myself seem worthy of help and being recognised as medically needing aid. I had to change my behaviour around nurses and doctors who I strongly disliked because of their treatment of me and had to make myself falsely sweet and childlike, changing my voice to be softer, more saccharine, desperate. I asked my parents to bring in edible treats to hand out to carers so they would look after me better and reduce the abusive and neglectful treatment.

I asked myself how a situation that was meant to be my saving grace, an admission into hospital to receive care for an increasingly sickening body, had turned into a fight for survival? Not against the disease itself but a fight for the clinicians to care for me, to see me as a young, incredibly frail girl who was desperate to be respected or, if not that, at least treated as a human being in a terrifying situation.

After reaching a point in my health where I was briefly well enough to access higher education I was excited at the chance of a new life. This feeling was cut painfully short. I was once again met by the stark reality of the work I had to do to be accepted as my disabled self, carrying the health conditions I have. I thought I had already earned my place at medical school, little did I know that I would have to work to be recognised as good enough to be there. My disability and health conditions were misrepresented as a barrier. I was seen as 'the other', unworthy of equal treatment to my peers. This was not what I thought a centre of healthcare teaching would be. I thought my previous hospital experience was a one off, a terrible mistake. The next few years at medical school were incredibly difficult. The combination of the medical school and opinions of medics in my new town (both GP and 'so-called' specialists), once again forced me into a position of deep shame and despair. The position I found myself in isn't unique to me, as Marks (1999) and Thomas (1999) note, the treatment of disabled people at the hands of the medical profession can also have adverse effects on their emotional wellbeing, leaving them feeling ashamed, vulnerable and objectified (Marks 1999; Thomas, 1999).

I felt like I was constantly fighting. Fighting for my body to keep working, fighting to prove myself as being worthy of becoming a doctor and fighting the doctors and teachers to accept me and my diagnoses. I thought I had already earned my place at medical school, little did I know that I would have to fight (futilely) to earn respect and a feeling of worthiness.

The level of work needed to get into medical school was far outstripped by that needed for acceptance and recognition, which was deeply traumatising. This fight for acceptance and recognition in medical spaces should not be underestimated, nor should its deep emotional effects, as reflected by the labour disabled young people undertake to justify themselves and their place in society. It has taken many years of continually working, advocating and educating myself to get to the point where I understand and agree with my diagnoses. I can explain them better than anyone else to medical professionals (if they are willing to listen) and after years of battle and protest I now get the care that I need. However, this has taken a tremendous toll emotionally, physically and psychologically and the amount of work I have had to do has been overwhelming. For some disabled young people, every moment is a labour to survive. The work that disabled young people undertake can be an acute pressure that they face daily or can even be considered as the work they have to do to stay alive, for air to enter and leave their bodies.

SOCIAL CARE, EMOTIONAL LABOUR AND ADVOCACY

We can also see Co-researcher Sally's emotional labour as a form of advocacy work. Advocacy work, or speaking up for yourself, is a role disabled people and their families are often forced to take on (Ryan and Runswick-Cole, 2008). Not speaking up seriously risks being denied required support. At times, a person's life may even depend on them being able to advocate for themselves.

Sally, like Ruth, has had to become, not only the expert of her illnesses and own body, but also says: I've had to educate myself how to convince the health care sector *and* the social care sector *and* those around me to listen to me and provide me with what I need. In so doing, I have had to become my own advocate, which is yet another form of emotional labour. It feels like this work will never end. This feeling was also described by the disabled young people who participated in our project.

Ramesh describes the work to get his needs met and highlights that this puts him off asking for support:

> *At the moment I don't have 24 hour care, I think I kind of want a bit more ... the strain on them [his parents], I know it's quite tiring and ... my mum just kind of soldiers on ... I know obviously I would get more care ... but then you have to fight for more hours.*

Similarly, Co-researcher Sally recalls: I remember a period of time where my bedroom (the only place that I had access to as I was living on the top floor of a house with stairs) functioned not only as my bathroom and dining room but also as a busy office and the headquarters of a campaign and battle ground, when it was supposed to be a place of rest and recuperation. For hours on end, my carer and I would make phone calls, send emails, arrange appointments and trawl the internet to gain access to suitable housing, find and secure consultations with the right specialists, set in place my care package, chase medication and access benefits. My support worker told me it was the hardest she had ever worked. Every hour was consumed by working to get the support to meet my needs. All of this labour was interspersed with fortnightly trips to London by ambulance to see more specialists, collect more diagnoses and experiment with new treatments. I was exhausted. I remember wondering how anyone (who did not have the support of a carer or family as I did) could carry the load of so much work alone when so unwell and I genuinely believe that others may not have survived under such a burden. I grieved for them. This was a stark realisation of what 'labour' was and that this form of work really made the difference between life and death.

Likewise, Co-researcher Katy explains: advocacy work has forced me into a role I do not think I would otherwise take on. I am not a naturally assertive person and highly value my privacy. However, in a quest to get support I have had to become someone I am not. It has been necessary to familiarise myself with laws and policies, learn how services work, chase professionals and repeatedly justify my 'needs'. In my attempt to negotiate support, I have often been caught between services and felt like a human pass the parcel whom no-one was willing to take notice of. It can be disheartening because it feels like there is always another battle around the corner and I can never fully relax. The ever present threat of austerity cuts is constantly there and with it, the uncomfortable reminder that my life is in the control of others.

Disabled people's insight into how their life could be improved is not always valued by professionals or the policies they are governed by. Disabled people are, too often, required to bow to the 'expertise' of professionals and to read their lives through the lens of deficit, lack and pathology (Rabinow and Rose, 2006). This happens despite the fact that disabled people often have creative and person-centred solutions to enable them to live full lives as shown by Helen and Josh:

> [...] look at the individual and 'what's right for this individual', 'how can we use this bit of money we have to meet the needs of this individual in quite a creative way', is the way forward and thinking a bit more holistically.

However, this is not always the case in practice as Anna highlights:

> The way that they have changed the emphasis on how Direct Payments should be spent/used, they seem to me to be ignoring a disabled person's overall wellbeing, placing more of an emphasis simply on social care. Which I suppose is vital, but I do find this rather frustrating when I ask them whether I can spend the money on something else, which I regard as being very beneficial to me, but then they say no to that.

Managing within the allocated resources can be a source of stress and frustration and may lead to disabled young people being forced to prioritise some areas over others despite them being equally important as Anna further describes:

> If I used personal carers more and paid for their services, I would have less [Direct Payment] money to be able to afford good PAs [personal assistants] to help me with my studies. It's quite difficult to get the balance right when spending one's limited resources/money.

For Co-researcher Katy, the process of assessments involves a forced level of intimacy (Mingus, 2017) she wishes she did not have to sacrifice.

Non-disabled people are not subjected to the countless times I have been expected to tell strangers intimate details or justify why the life I wish to live *cannot* and *should not* shrink into the constrictive allocated hours where support is available. I have felt violated by this intrusion into my personal life by someone I would not choose to share these details with. In these processes my divergence from the ableist norm (Goodley, 2014) is made painfully obvious and leaves me stripped bare (Marks, 1999). I have even been left questioning my worth as a human being. It takes a huge amount of emotional labour to think about all the difficulties I experience in minute detail whilst still holding onto a positive sense of self. Emotional labour impacts on what disabled people can do and who they can be (Thomas, 1999).

All these assessments focussed on me and my impairment. They rarely, if ever, addressed the external barriers that make my life difficult. Consequently, I spent my first 17 years of life thinking *I* was the problem. Being introduced to the social model liberated me from the burden I did not know I was carrying. I share this feeling with the disabled feminist Liz Crow (1996) who declared:

> *My life has two phases: before the social model of disability, and after it. Discovering this way of thinking about my experiences was the proverbial raft in stormy seas. It gave me an understanding of my life, shared with thousands, even millions, of other people around the world, and I clung to it. (p. 55)*

Whilst individual advocacy work can feel frustrating and isolating, reaching out to the disability community has given me hope and kept my flame burning despite the many threats to extinguish it. I learned that I have rights and I am entitled to have these honoured.

For many participants, the outcome of their advocacy work was to be given personal budgets to employ PAs. We have discussed the emotional labour of being recipients of support in Chapter 4.

Employing PAs also brings additional work in terms of recruiting and managing a team, often with little training or external support. This is very different from the conventional world of work where people are likely to move into management after building up some experience beforehand. Jane described this sudden responsibility as being daunting: 'I didn't know what the hell I was doing a lot of the time but it was suddenly I had that responsibility and a legal responsibility'. Jane also described the pressure of managing both her and her PA's needs:

*There is all of the arranging like them wanting to go on holiday but
yet at the same time you would love to let them take that holiday
but you don't have any cover so you have to say no.*

Co-researcher Katy reflects on how employing PAs can feel like running a
24/7 HR service with no downtime: Not having conventional working hours
will mean I will get a text at 11 p.m. asking for annual leave which not only
throws up practical issues but can be a source of emotional labour in itself.
Thus, I have experienced this need to keep PAs 'on side'. I feel PA work is
often not seen as a long career and I am hyper aware they could leave at any
moment which is painful when I have established trust with someone. It is
also another instance of the power imbalance and not being in control of my
life. Sometimes when a PA leaves it has put me in fight/flight mode, knowing I
have to find someone else because if I cannot arrange cover I won't be able to
eat or wash. No matter what I have happening in my life, everything must go
on hold and recruitment is my full-time task. Recruitment can be another act
of forced intimacy – putting my needs in adverts and into the public domain
which have attracted inappropriate comments and harassment and then
having to go through these tasks in detail at each interview.

Participants reported being simultaneously grateful for the support and
independence it gave them but also acknowledging the extra workload of
employing PAs. This work is undertaken in intimate spaces such as homes
where there is no escape from it. As Rachel summarised: 'Whilst it's their job,
it's my life …'.

CRIPPING THE WORKPLACE

Disability activists and disability studies academics have often engaged with
labour as a key concern of disabled people (Bates et al., 2017). Social model
scholars have long argued that disabled people want to work but are not
allowed to (Oliver, 1996). In co-researchers Sally and Katy's discussion of
emotional labour and advocacy work, we see the ways in which disabled
people are constructed as objects of labour (and subjects of care) at the same
time as they have been made unemployable – the workplace is, all too often,
constructed as a space where disabled people are 'out of place' and unable to
meet the demands of ableist normativity that are deeply embedded in working environments (Bates et al., 2017; Kitchin, 1998). Bodies and minds which
cannot bend or flex to meet the clock are, ultimately, excluded from the (paid)
workplace (Kafer, 2013). As a signifier of valued citizenship, exclusion from
paid work has devastating impacts on the lives of disabled people who become

ever more reliant on the (shrinking) resources of the welfare state (Goodley, 2016). Ten years of austerity in Britain, followed by a pandemic which has disproportionately impacted on disabled people (Shakespeare et al., 2021), means that disabled people are finding it harder than ever to find work when opportunities for labour are scarce for everyone.

And, for those disabled people who are in work, the workplace can be a space where disabled young people experience forms of marginalisation, discrimination and exclusion. As Co-researcher Katy says: What is reasonable to one person may not be to another. I experienced this in a past employment. The team I was part of were based upstairs in a building with no lift. The desks downstairs were all in use so the reasonable adjustment my employer made was to buy a desk and put in the stationary cupboard. I was eager to please and be seen as a hardworking employee so I made an effort to get on with it. As time went on I felt more isolated from my team whom I only saw in weekly meetings. I would hear snippets of banter but I was always on the perimeter. I had queries to run past my colleagues but I didn't want to keep exchanging emails upstairs – I just wanted to be able to chat to them from my desk. I began raising my concerns in supervision. I was told I just had to phone them and someone would come down and 'keep me company'. I tried this a couple of times but felt guilty that I was putting my colleagues out. It is true I was given a desk which didn't require me to negotiate stairs. However, I was excluded from my team and resources which made my job practically challenging. It also left me feeling isolated and questioning my role within the team.

Katy's account reveals the ways in which spaces construct disabled people as 'other'. At the same time as she was made to feel 'out of place', she was also 'put in her place' (in the stationary cupboard), revealing her employer's assumption that disabled employees should simply tolerate inappropriate working environments, and leaving Katy with the emotional labour of managing the feelings of colleagues 'keeping her company'. Rather than challenging the exclusion, in Hochschild's (1983) terms, Katy was forced to be nicer than natural.

Katy's story challenges us to think differently about work and to imagine crip alternatives to narrow, ableist conceptions of work underpinned by normative notions of time and space.

Finding Crip Alternatives

Here, we reflect on the ways in which it is possible to crip the workplace, drawing on our research project itself to explore the ways in which a crip workplace is an accessible and inclusive workplace for all.

We start with a reminder that under the The Equality Act 2010 disabled people have rights in relation to employment. The Equality Act requires employers to have in mind the varying needs of (potential) employees at all times and to make 'reasonable adjustments' for them. Meeting these legal obligations means embracing crip alternatives: employees cannot simply ignore disabled people in the workplace or expect them to conform to perceived to be able-bodied norms (McRuer, 2006).

As we say earlier in the chapter, we reject the view that human value can or should be equated to productivity in the workplace. Nonetheless, we do need to challenge negative representations of disabled employees. Disabled people are no more or less likely to be 'good' or 'bad' employees as anyone else. As we see below, adjustments made for disabled people, such as accessible resources and flexible working, actually have benefits for all employees. Supporting disabled people into employment is also associated with lower overall costs to the state. The National Audit Office (2011) report Oversight of Special Education for Young People Aged 16–25 estimates that supporting one person with a learning disability into employment could, in addition to improving their independence and self-esteem, reduce lifetime costs to the public purse by around £170,000 and increase the person's income by between 55% and 95%. Similarly, Hunter et al. (2019) suggest that providing young people with the relevant life and employability skills so that they can live in their community could reduce lifetime support costs to the public by approximately £1 million. In other words, however critical we may be of the logic of neoliberalism, there is a business case for crip alternatives in the workplace.

Of course, accessible workspaces need to be physically accessible but crip inclusivity goes way beyond adaptations to the physical environment. Crip workplaces are flexible in terms of time and space. Flexibility can include working from home for some of the week, starting later in the day or taking an extended break. All employees have a legal right to request flexible working and employers must deal with requests in a 'reasonable manner' (Equality Act 2010). Flexibility can be very useful for a number of types of employees, including parents, older employees and those with caring roles. Despite employers' fears about offering flexible working it has been shown to increase employee commitment to an organisation and an employee's focus on their work (Clarke and Holdsworth, 2017).

Too often there is an assumption that to be a good employee, you have to be able to sit in the office from nine to five. A crip orientation leads us to trouble this assumption. Writing as we do in the middle of the Covid-19 pandemic lock down, we have seen the benefits of the vast number of changes that have been made to enable people to work from home, including utilising virtual technologies. The Covid-19 pandemic created the need for just the kinds of flexible working that have so often been denied to disabled people in the past (Hirst and Foster, 2021). The moment of disruption that Covid-19 has brought us has demonstrated the necessity for crip alternative workspaces. Post-Covid, the challenge will be to protect and develop these crip alternatives rather than lapsing back into 'normal' working practices premised on notions of ablebodiedness (McRuer, 2006).

We now move to share our learning as colleagues working on The Living Life to the Fullest Project and describe some of the ways in which we attempted to *crip* our workplace to enhance accessibility for all members of the research team.

Crip Alternative One – Accessible Spaces

From the beginning of the research project, we quickly came to realise that we needed to find accessible spaces. We were presented with huge challenges in bringing together a team that was divided by geographical location, but also other calls on our time, which included, as we've seen, managing medical care and social care, but also our caring responsibilities and other relationships. It very rapidly became clear that being in the same room was not going to be possible. Even in pre-Covid times, we welcomed disability for the disruptive potential it brought to us thinking about how we were going to work together. We began to hold meetings online and used shared virtual documents to communicate ideas between meetings, and, indeed, to write this book. We worked from our kitchens, sitting rooms, bedrooms and even from our beds – whatever worked for each of us.

Despite the success of these remote approaches, The Co-Researcher Collective wanted to be together in real life as well as in virtual spaces. We responded to this urge to meet in the real world (again, this will be very familiar to readers in the context of Covid-19) by searching out accessible spaces to meet. This was a massive challenge. Whilst hotels and conference rooms might have a couple of accessible rooms, finding a space that could accommodate The Co-Researcher Collective in the same space at the same time was a huge challenge that took a lot of work to mediate.

Crip Alternative Two – Accessible Times

We thought about the times of our meetings to fit in with the team members' daily routines and commitments, cameras and microphones were turned off whilst the phlebotomist came to take blood, or to take a phone call from the consultant. We also made sure that meetings were not too long and were mindful of the pace of online meetings, which we all now know can be overwhelming. We wanted people to be able to work at the times that were best for them and that allowed people to take rest when they needed to, but to be able to work when they wanted to, too. For some of us, a regular routine helped us to keep on track, but for others work happened between appointments and spells of fatigue, illness and hospitalisation.

Crip Alternative Three – Accessible Technology

We could not have done this project without access to technology. We all depended heavily on online video meetings and shared online documents. Email and WhatsApp allowed us to communicate in our own time and at our own pace.

Co-researcher Sally used assistive technology to help her to dictate into a headset rather than using a keyboard to type. Text to speech software allowed her to listen to information, rather than reading. This meant that she was able to receive large amounts of information whilst lying in bed, working for longer periods of time and using energy for creative outputs as opposed to using it to physically cope with merely taking in data.

We were all aware of our privileged access to both the hardware and software that allowed us to work together and are mindful that this is not a privilege that has been granted to all disabled people who remain amongst the most digitally excluded members of society (Yu et al., 2019).

Crip Alternative Four – Accessible Systems

Working on the project shone a spotlight on the barriers that government policy and employers' systems can present to disabled employees. These issues are clearly illustrated by the story of one of the members of The Co-Researcher Collective. We have chosen not to identify her here for purposes of anonymity. Her story is as follows:

This project work was my first foray into the workplace since being a teenager and I was happy doing it unpaid. I came to realise that my experience as a disabled young person has value, is considered to be knowledge and in fact brings something to the research. However, when I was offered the opportunity to be paid for some of the research, I immediately encountered problems. Firstly, at the level of government policy and second at the level of the systems employers use. In order for me to do paid work, I've had to face the difficulty of navigating the benefits system which has been stressful, labour intensive and ultimately felt risky. I receive a benefit called employment and support allowance (ESA) because my disability and health condition affect how much I can do and therefore prevent me from undertaking a full-time job. However, under a scheme called 'Permitted work' I am allowed to do some work, which is capped at a set number of hours and pay per week. Yet, I could find no official information about how the impact of putting in for 'Permitted work' may affect the likelihood of how soon I might be reassessed for ESA. I also worried about whether it would affect my personal independence payment (PIP) benefit, my main source of income; losing this would be disastrous.

I managed to work out from other disabled people in work and online that *theoretically* it shouldn't affect these benefits, yet I had no reassurance from the professionals of this – even when speaking directly to the Department for Work and Pensions (DWP). They provided no guarantees, gave mixed messages and even told me that they thought the idea of being on ESA but being able to do 'some' limited work was paradoxical! Nonetheless, I ploughed on as I knew the value of the work and satisfaction it was giving me.

This was when I encountered my second problem: how the system of the University treated me as an employee and paid me accordingly. It seemed, once again, that the current system was unable to accommodate my way of working as a disabled person who was also claiming benefits. I was considered a casual worker and asked to put in monthly timesheets. However, the nature of project work and payroll system meant that I was sometimes paid lump sums of money for work undertaken over several months. To the DWP, this looked like I was doing more hours per week than I was permitted (despite this not being the case). There is no system in place for disabled people who undertake project work on an ad hoc basis and receive benefits to be paid weekly by the University, which would have prevented the DWP's concerns. The system is set up for people who are able to do a contracted job that pays per annum.

This led to a high degree of anxiety since the DWP investigated me for potentially fraudulently claiming benefits. Not only was this incredibly stressful, as I risked losing both my ESA, PIP and faced fraud allegations, but also involved a large amount of labour on my part: it took hours trying to sort out the payment schedule so that it would meet the permitted work scheme requirements. I had to explain everything to the University, have a continual back and forth with the payroll department AND provide solid evidence to the DWP that I was only working small amounts. It caused me to question whether doing the work that I was physically able to do, and that brought me so much joy, was actually worth it if it was going to cause me so much time and emotional labour to justify myself.

I found myself bending to a system that would not bend for me in a context where, as a disabled person 'in work', I was considered to be 'out of place' and felt 'put in my place' by the possibility of a fraud investigation. Crip alternative workspaces need flexible systems that do not discriminate against different ways of working.

Crip Alternative Five – Accessible Cultures

Crip alternative workplaces depend on accessible environments and technologies, but, crucially, they also require culture change. All employees need to feel empowered to be confident to discuss their own personal needs, and reasonable adjustments, without fear of judgement.

In the project, we hoped to create a culture in which disability was always viewed as a valuable resource and every moment of disruption was taken up as an opportunity to think differently about how we could work together. We worked as a Collective which meant that when members of the team experienced periods of ill health, or were absent because of other commitments, other members of the Collective could pick up the work and carry on. Sharing all documents online helped us to do this. And so, as it turned out when Covid-19 hit, our crip workplace had prepared us well.

CONCLUSION

In our writing this chapter, we were drawn again and again to the complexity of labour in the lives of disabled young people that so often goes unrecognised, even by disabled young people themselves. Writing the chapter has made us all pay attention to the types of labour we are engaging with, including emotional labour, and the spaces that labour occurs in – homes, hospitals and the community – as well as in more formal workspaces. We are also struck by the need to bend time, rather than bodies, in crip workspaces. We conclude by calling for a recognition of labour in the lives of disabled young people that means that, too often, there is no home time and no home space.

8

MAKING MEANINGFUL IMPACT IN AND WITH SCHOOLS

GREENACRE CO-RESEARCHERS: JEMMA, MARCONI, LOGAN, ALEX, STEVIE AND EMILY; HARRY GORDON AND KIRSTY LIDDIARD

ACCESSIBLE SUMMARY

- In this short chapter, we share another collaboration to emerge from The Living Life to the Fullest Project, with Greenacre School, Barnsley.
- We discuss a small impact project called *What Matters?*
- We highlight access to research and inquiry as an exciting form of learning and teaching.
- We talk about our co-production toolkit, *Why Can't We Dream?*

INTRODUCTION

This chapter explores the ways in which The Living Life to the Fullest sought to expand its networks and experiences of co-producing research with disabled children and young people. While we are proud of the political and practical collaborative emphases across our work, we do note that our co-researchers in The Co-Researcher Collective are all young women aged 18+, White, middle class, living with life-limiting and life-threatening impairments, and over half have been educated to university level. Therefore, our co-production processes inevitably benefit from co-researchers' own abilities, privileges, skills and knowledge (see Whitney et al., 2019). We wanted to explore the ways in which we might expand our co-production practices to other disabled young people in other contexts. In 2017, we began a collaboration with Greenacre School, Barnsley. Greenacre is a school educating children and young people aged 3–19 labelled with severe and complex needs. The school became an Academy in April 2015 and subsequently joined the Wellspring Academy Trust in April 2017. It was a chance meeting – we were fortunate enough to connect with Harry Gordon, a special educational need and disability (SEND) teacher from Greenacre, at an Economic and Social Research Council (ESRC) Festival of Social Sciences event we were running with The Co-Researcher Collective on co-production and accessible research.

Harry attended the event because he had an existing interest in researching with young people at Greenacre and had been conducting a project with his students called The Loneliness Project. The aim of The Loneliness Project was to explore young people's experiences of loneliness. The group of students working on The Loneliness Project later presented findings from the project which influenced Barnsley Council to change the way they produce research. Sharing findings from the project with Barnsley Safeguarding Children's Partnership Board, Heads of Service and Commissioners, as well as representatives from each of the safeguarding partners (Police, Social Care and Clinical Commissioning Group) and relevant partner agencies, evidenced that students could not only share their experiences of loneliness, but affect meaningful change. Co-researcher Logan said of co-producing research with Harry on loneliness, 'I was really shocked by how many people felt lonely. I really enjoyed sharing our research at the council at the Town Hall'. Yet, Harry was really struck by the Living Life to the Fullest Project and its positioning of young people as leading and shaping every stage of the research process. Harry was keen to explore how he could use this philosophy and approach to collaboratively conduct further research with young people in his own classroom. This connection led to a fruitful and exploratory relationship through which we took our co-production methods into the SEND classroom, building new researcher relationships with children and young people with labels of learning disability and autism through a small Living Life to the Fullest impact project called, *What Matters?*

In this chapter, co-authored by Harry, Kirsty and our *What Matters?* co-researchers (hereby Greenacre co-researchers) – Jemma, Marconi, Logan, Alex, Stevie and Emily – we share how we have worked together and what we have learned as collaborators across different educational contexts. We focus on creating an accessible research education and open research process. We attend to the desires of Greenacre co-researchers to have influence over the decisions within the research process and on being and becoming researchers within inquiry about their own lives. This chapter also speaks to the ways in which we've found that accessing research supports the work of both students and teachers, not only meeting and recording students' educational targets but offering a more creative and empowering curriculum through engaging in research. We also show the ways in which Greenacre co-researchers accessed and entered the university – through leading their own ESRC Festival event and coming into the university to work alongside academics. We end this chapter by advocating the benefits of our co-production toolkit, *Why Can't We Dream?*

ENACTING INQUIRY: WORKING IN SCHOOL

Through a series of fun and engaging Research Workshops we worked with Greenacre co-researchers at the school to co-produce a small research project that sought to explore what matters to students at Greenacre: what they like, what they dislike and what's important to them. Greenacre co-researchers undertook research training (we share these approaches below), learning about asking questions, data collection, ethics and methods of analysis. They then collected data from one another and together we undertook a collaborative analysis. Sadly, our research process was cut short due to the Covid-19 pandemic and the closure of schools. Our original plan had been for Greenacre co-researchers to collect data from the wider student body at the school via qualitative and quantitative methods, and we had ethical approval from the School of Education Ethics Committee to do so, but because of the way we were restricted in relation to risk and safety, we had to settle with the data we had already collected from within the team. Understandably, both the Covid-19 pandemic-related closures of schools and the subsequent recovery period for schools and universities has been a key barrier in the process. Much of the latter meant that our time and focus as educators and researchers was elsewhere, and our capacity and time was diminished.

In session one, we began by introducing the concept of research – What is it? What does it *do*? Why does it matter? We began with Harry's concept of The Big Question (see Illustration 1). Our Greenacre co-researchers collectively chose a big question – *What matters to you?* We then used creative methods to explore answers to this question from the perspectives of young people. Next, we worked back from this question, asking what types of 'smaller' questions might you ask others to explore a range of different answers to The Big Question. The Big Question approach involves a range of stages to unpack and explore an area or topic. Each stage has a purpose to make space, give time and to work together in collaboration to explore. To give an example, Harry advocates 'silent time'. This might be actioned as a minute's silent reflection. We found that this approach to critical thinking with young people mediates the 'need' to respond or perform straight away, giving deeper and more considered responses to the question. We also brought in objects to stimulate discussion into new areas. For example, we brought to the introductory session objects that represented hobbies and passions that mattered to us. We then instigated a sensorial discussion – touching, smelling, playing with the stimulus/objects – as a way *into* deeper discussion about what we cherished and why. Questions that emerged in this session included: Why do we live? What do you think is the best thing in life? What is the scariest thing in life for you? Why do we get up in the morning?

In session two, we began to work on ways that our future participants could *answer* questions – *how* would we enable them to answer – and through what means or methods. We began with a recap of the last session, followed by a short activity designed to think again about ways of asking questions. Using small speech bubble cards with different words on, such as: How? Why? When? Explain. Tell me a story. Demonstrate. Define (available

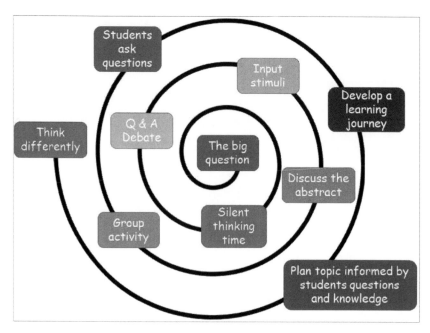

Illustration 1.   Image Description: Designed by Harry Gordon, SEND Teacher, Greenacre School, this diagram shows our methods of how we explored the notion of developing questions for an interview schedule.

to download on the *Why Can't We Dream?* Toolkit), we sat in a group and designed different types of questions. This work served to further develop our earlier questions. For example, discussions stimulated by the activity led to more in-depth and specific questions Greenacre co-researchers wanted to ask their participants. These included questions such as: Is it OK to be LGBT? and if you see someone getting picked on, what will you do?

In session three, in response to our need to obtain further institutional ethics approval, beyond what we already had for The Living Life to the Fullest Project, we began to focus on the meaning of ethics. We didn't want the ethics process to be only the task 'the adults' managed as part of the process (see Nind et al., 2012). Ethics, as a subject, can be dry, complex and conceptual. Our desire to want to explain in an accessible way was, for us, a key barrier in the process. However, we overcame this: to support young people's understanding of what ethics means in practice within research, we decided to make it accessible, fun and creative. Harry devised a series of activities – an ethics assault course – whereby Greenacre co-researchers worked through different obstacles that helped consider different facets of ethical considerations: confidentiality, information safety, time, costs (emotional and financial) and protection from harm (Illustration 2). We did this through differentiation, lots of objects, visual prompts, objects of reference and activity-based assault courses. We used PE equipment to set up challenges. Each challenge

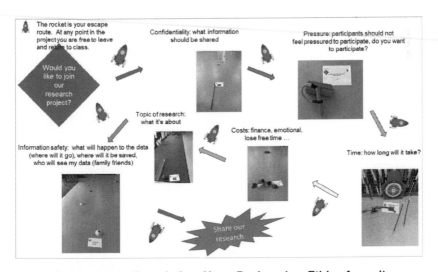

Illustration 2.   Image Description: Harry Designed an Ethics Assault Course, set out in the school hall, through which Greenacre co-researchers could play with and learn about ethical considerations in research. All of the activities were made accessible for all children, regardless of disability, impairment and/or label.

represented different stages of the ethics process, exploring different ethical dilemmas that Greenacre co-researchers related to their own everyday experiences (e.g. talking about the future was exciting for some co-researchers, while others shared their experiences of anxiety when thinking about leaving home).

Following this, we sat down to discuss different 'ethical dilemmas' that spoke to young people's everyday experiences: for example, *a friend tells you that they have a girlfriend in class but they don't want you to tell anyone.* We also included some scenarios related specifically to the research methods they were about to undertake with their peers: for example, *when interviewing students someone tells you about how they are feeling lonely, what action, if any, do you take?* As a group, we took our time to discuss these dilemmas, thinking about it from a variety of different perspectives. In time, we had co-built an interview schedule for use in our data collection. Working inclusively with students with a variety of needs allowed us to make sure that co-production was accessible to all Greenacre co-researchers, paying attention to students working at a different levels of ability as defined in SEND contexts. Harry's philosophy was that, whatever 'stage' or 'ability' young people are at, through creativity and exploration, everyone can participate in co-produced research ethically and authentically.

WORKING IN AND WITH THE UNIVERSITY

We agreed early on that it was very important for Greenacre co-researchers to come to the university. Thus, in late 2017 we all participated in an Analysis Workshop which was held at the School of Education at the University of Sheffield. This offered an important opportunity for disabled young people in SEND schools, many of whom are routinely excluded from mainstream educational spaces, especially higher education, despite the inclusion agenda (see Klang et al., 2020). For us as a Research Team it was equally important to treat Greenacre co-researchers the same as we would any other colleague or partner. Our Greenacre co-researchers share their experiences below:

Stevie: *It made me feel more mature.*

Jemma: *It helped to build my confidence.*

Alex: *It was a unique experience alongside my friends.*

Emily: *It was good to go somewhere different, my brother is now at Sheffield University.*

Inevitably, coming to the university took some planning – we had to produce risk assessments, notify fellow colleagues of our plans, seek permission from our Head of School, as well as plan the security and fire evacuation practicalities for having young people on site. We scheduled a day with lots of space to relax in unfamiliar surroundings; we ordered a good lunch; and we based much of our analytical work on the day around play: using Lego, building blocks and other materials to stimulate discussion and explore our data. We also thought about key ways we wanted to represent our data once analysed: How can we be inclusive in terms of telling others about our key findings? We had the idea to co-create 3D representations of findings – ways to communicate what matters to young people without producing a lengthy, inaccessible report.

PRESENTING OUR WORK

In November 2019, together we won some funding to host an ESRC Festival of Social Sciences Event. The ESRC Festival of Social Science is a celebration of the social sciences. At our event, it was key that Greenacre co-researchers were the main presenters. This had a profound impact on co-researchers' parents as well as for our co-researchers. For example, Jemma's Mum said she loved talking to university students after the festival event and that she hadn't had the chance to do this before. She beamed at how proud she was of Jemma, and that it was positive that parents got to contribute at the event as well. Similarly, Marconi's Mum said:

> it was amazing to see so many people with disabilities at the festival of social science. It gave Marconi a voice. Marconi really enjoyed the whole process and didn't stop talking about it all the way home from the festival event.

Thus, this was a powerful opportunity and experience for all; our Greenacre co-researchers share their thoughts below:

> Stevie: It was scary to start with because I thought there were too many people, but I got used to it and got more confident.

> Jemma: I was shocked at first (doing the activities) but then I felt happy once I had learned what to do.

> Alex: This was a one time learning opportunity that not many would have. But definitely one that I'd like to repeat.

> Emily: It was exciting and it made me feel happy.

However, it's important to acknowledge that for some co-researchers this was very comfortable – being nervous was, understandably, a collective experience – while for others we had to think of alternative ways to be involved in ways that were preferred, safe and accessible:

Emily: I learnt how to present in front of other people.

Jemma: I got better at not being nervous.

Stevie: I managed feeling nervous.

Alex: At first it was weird watching other people but it was OK once I was actually doing it.

Logan: The event at the Festival of Social Science was the first time I had spoken to a big audience and it was nerve-wracking but I got used to it. I would do it again. This helped my confidence to speak up in front of a crowd. I am proud of myself.

Our aim, then, was for Greenacre co-researchers to have space, with a varied audience, to talk about their project. We also wanted to show how we worked together, outline our methods and affirm to others the importance of undertaking research in meaningful ways with disabled young people in SEND environments. Greenacre co-researchers, and their parents and carers, noted that it was like nothing else they had ever experienced. We saw a distinct growth in confidence with all Greenacre co-researchers, and many parents, sharing their explorations intimately and authentically.

WHY CAN'T WE DREAM? A CO-PRODUCTION TOOLKIT

The approaches we have outlined in this chapter form a key part of our co-production toolkit, *Why Can't We Dream?* It is a significant legacy from the Living Life to the Fullest Project, and our work with community partners and schools. Our aim is that it will both impact and reshape the way research happens with all disabled young people in the future, across a variety of contexts. It's totally free to use and share. The toolkit is full of interactive resources as well as details of our co-production process, with The Co-Researcher Collective, with schools and communities, and across the arts and virtual spaces. The toolkit contains all of our films, podcasts, articles and tools that we've built throughout the lifecycle of the project.

LEARNING AND ASSESSMENT

Related to our collaboration with Greenacre, we see the toolkit as particularly useful in relation to embedding research into schools. In the toolkit, Harry has created lesson plans, PowerPoint resources and activities that are free and accessible for teachers and schools to use, share and embed in their own classrooms. We see research as an empowering pedagogical tool: ways for students to take ownership of their learning through inquiry and useful for teachers to undertake a variety of different activities with students in ways that support the recording of their learning and targets centred in SEND curricula. For example, Harry further used *What Matters?* to document the journey of student development through the project. He was able to capture the impacts on students' progress in numeracy, literacy and emotional wellbeing measured at Greenacre School through Personalised Learning Map targets. These document students' development in core subjects as well as life skills and Education Health and Care Plan targets. He was able to explore, as an educator, the ways in which research and inquiry can make space to develop abstract thinking skills and creative exploration. Moreover, Harry witnessed how access to research participation and leadership supported co-researchers with what are known as 'higher order thinking skills' in relation to Bloom's taxonomy (Bloom, 1956), hierarchical models used to classify educational learning objectives into levels of remember, understand, apply, analyse, evaluate and create. It was insightful to see how co-researchers *used* empathy and their own experiences to understand complex issues around ethics. It was also interesting how students developed more philosophical and deeper questions during the research process. For example, Greenacre co-researcher Alex started to develop ideas about how disability can have some benefits and can be a part of 'who we are'. Thus, co-researchers were given accessible and safe spaces to think 'outside the box', to navigate complex obstacles and challenges.

CONCLUSION

In this chapter, co-authored by Harry and Greenacre co-researchers – Jemma, Marconi, Logan, Alex, Stevie and Emily – we have shared our preliminary forays into the impact research and inquiry can have in SEND educational contexts, and the creative ways in which this can happen. Introducing the politics of co-production to SEND spaces and curricula is important for schools and for children and young people. We advocate that research can be powerfully centred within SEND pedagogy. We were early into our collaboration when Covid-19 hit, so we are yet to fully finish *What Matters?* although we are proud to have it included in this book. We also want to emphasise the benefits where academics and educational professionals and schools work together and suggest that these partnerships make important contributions to critical disability studies and disabled children's childhood studies research (see Runswick-Cole et al., 2018). We share much of our process in our co-production toolkit, *Why Can't We Dream?* Please feel free to visit the toolkit online and access all of the available resources.

9

DESIRING LIFE AND LIVING WITH DEATH

KATY EVANS, SALLY WHITNEY-MITCHELL AND KIRSTY LIDDIARD

ACCESSIBLE SUMMARY

- In this chapter, we talk about the difficult topics of death and dying.
- We argue that research hasn't talked to disabled young people about death enough.
- We explore living life fully, illness, the future, and grief and legacy.
- We end by stating that being remembered is very important to disabled young people living short/er lives.

INTRODUCTION

This chapter was always going to be one of the hardest to write. Throughout the project, disabled children and young people living with life-threatening and life-limiting impairments (LL/LTIs), and with shortened life expectancies, have readily emphasised their human worth, value, and desire for the future – regardless of how long these futures might be. Moreover, they have done so in disabling cultures that routinely deny them opportunity, access, and expectation. Young people have also stressed the ways in which they routinely thrive and strive in often difficult circumstances. Death and dying have, understandably, been difficult topics to approach in a project that focusses on affirming the value of and joy in the lives of disabled children and young people. We've talked about emotional work and labour (Hochschild, 1983) throughout this book – the notion that feeling and processing emotion, both internally on the self and on the surface, is a form of affective work. We reiterate it again here because talking about death and dying as a team (while living short/er lives), and also with our participants, was undeniably a space of extensive emotional work. Understandably, we found that in our interviews with young people there was a lack of explicitness in talking about death and dying. In our Analysis Retreat, we reflected upon why this was, and realised that it was the result of our tentative questioning: we had been afraid of approaching death and dying in our conversations with disabled young people.

These conversations, and our interpretation of them, became more complex and laboured upon the onset of the Covid-19 global panic. Suddenly thrown into a moment where all lives became vulnerable – an already-lived reality of many of the disabled young people in our project – it was also a time where ableism and disablism were routinely shored up, determining some of the gravest threats to disabled children and young people and their families in modern times. As we have outlined in previous chapters, ableism can be understood as the material, cultural and political privileging of ability, sanity, rationality, physicality and cognition (Braidotti, 2013; Goodley, 2014); while disablism refers to the resultant oppressive treatment of disabled people (Liddiard and Slater, 2017). Disablism and ableism are often dual processes: more often than not, they work in conjunction, supporting one another (Liddiard, 2018a). Without doubt, we are living in deeply disablist and ableist times – even before the threat of a global pandemic. Ableism and disablism are ever present within contemporary society, where neoliberal and scientific rationalist ideologies thrive. Even more so currently, when global capitalism, global austerity and a global pandemic highlight the costs and undermine the (human) value of disabled people. The Co-Researcher Collective emphasised at this time that we are valuable and valued human beings. That we have meaningful lives worth protecting and saving. That we are at risk as much from disablism and ableism as we are Covid-19, or other forms of precarity. And that being vulnerable does not equate with being less than human. That, ultimately, ableism – both inside and outside the precarious context of crisis – readily dehumanises us and demarcates our lives as disposable.

So, while the pandemic and its relationship to vulnerability, risk and death are inevitably the elephant in the room in this chapter, we don't want these conversations of human worth to dominate young people's own stories of disability, death and dying, which were so boldly relayed to us in the project. Young people living with LL/LTIs already exist within an embodied vulnerability and proximity to death, and it is these experiences that we want to honour in this chapter. Therefore, in this chapter, we detail and discuss young people's stories of desiring life and living with death. We do so through the lens of crip time (Kafer, 2013): the recognition of (disabled) people's need for 'more time' and, in this case, reconsidering what the 'future' currently means to disabled young people living with LL/LTIs.

We begin the chapter by exploring the methodological precarities and promises of talking to disabled young people about fragility, illness, death and dying. Importantly, we expose young people's capacities to survive and thrive. We consider the meanings of threat, risk and illness in the lives of young people. Later, we contemplate what this means for the ways in which disabled young people with short/er lives plan for their futures and how they mediate concepts of 'life expectancy' and grief. Finally, to conclude this important chapter, and book, we consider legacy. To us and our disabled young participants, legacy is being remembered and leaving something to the world, to our communities, for our families and loved ones. Legacy is critical to feeling that our lives and contributions are of value; that our lives matter. This is one of the most important ways to affirm disabled lives as valuable, meaningful, memorable and, ultimately, always worth living.

METHODOLOGICAL CHOICES: ASKING QUESTIONS ABOUT LIFE AND DEATH

The Living Life to the Fullest Project purposefully explored the lives of disabled young people living with LL/LTIs in order to consider how young people and their families make sense of living short/er lives and what new forms of exclusion can come with this unique lived experience. Project co-researchers felt that this aspect of the project needed to make distinctions between what they described as the internal experience of illness and impairment and the external barriers which cause disability as a social oppression. Disabled feminists have critiqued the social model for focussing too much on the external experiences of disability (see Crow, 1996; Lonsdale, 1990; Thomas, 1999; Wendell, 1996; Liddiard, 2018a). When this happens, the very embodied effects of illness and impairment are silenced regardless of their impact, often continuing to influence a person's life despite the removal of disabling barriers. As we have shown throughout this book, disabled young people are clearly able to identify the barriers which define their disability experience, but also show how important it is to highlight the internal and embodied experiences of illness and impairment and how this too shapes their lives in myriad ways. We centre these experiences in this chapter.

Some of us started to explore disablism in death and dying long ago (Runswick-Cole, 2010), noting the 'offensive presence' death has sometimes represented in disability studies (Runswick-Cole, 2010, p. 813). We acknowledge that, as a field of study that politically affirms the value of disabled lives and seeks to distinguish disability from individual personal tragedy (Oliver, 1990), disability studies has consequently often overlooked the intimate politics of death and dying. Such exclusion is mirrored in Western cultures, which often sequest death to the silent, hidden and private realm (Chapple et al., 2015). In the Global North, death is largely constructed as 'failure' – the failure of individual bodies as well as the inability of medicine to save a life, which Co-researcher Sally explores below. It is relegated to hospitals and hospices, as the dying are removed from community and domestic spaces (Seymour, 1999). The death of a young person, for example, has always been imbued with tragedy. Yet, as Runswick-Cole (2010) suggests, a disabled young person already troubles symbolic meanings of Western childhood and youth as future, hopeful and innocent. As such, the death of a disabled young person is perceived differently from the death of their non-disabled counterparts. Their deaths are described as a release from suffering, and by extension, their parents' grief is constructed as different (Runswick-Cole 2010; see also Wood and Milo 2001). As Runswick-Cole (2010, pp. 815–816) argues, 'the tacit ableist assumptions which inform these analyses of the death of a disabled child must be challenged'.

To honour this call to challenge, then, in our project we felt it important to ask disabled young people living with LL/LTIs about death and dying. However, we were understandably hesitant to do so, partly because of the possible ethical considerations of asking such sensitive questions (and *to* young people), but also because very few researchers have done so before (Runswick-Cole, 2010). We did so carefully. We designed a distress protocol (Draucker et al., 2009) to help us recognise and manage distress; we co-authored questions as a research team made up of academics and disabled young co-researchers; and we costed counselling sessions into our budget for those participants that might need to access further support. Moreover, when we came to analyse stories, we did so in collaboration, bringing members of the team together at a residential Analysis Retreat, a methodological ethic of care that offered a chance to be together outside of virtual spaces. We wanted to sit *together, with* sensitive stories, and reflect upon their meanings, both to us as researchers but also for our participants and their families (see Chapter 3). This was an incredibly emotional experience – and one we feel that was only made possible through the intimacies, friendships and deep trust that had grown in our team through the project (see Chapter 1).

In early discussions about the interview schedule, The Co-Researcher Collective felt it important to consider the future, regardless of what the future held for the young people at the centre of our project. Thus, we had a desire to make space for disabled young people to 'say the unsayable'. We also acknowledge that these are difficult topics for all people, and that an exceptional amount of trust and time is needed to talk about such issues. People often withhold deeper things until trust is established, especially in a research context (Liddiard, 2018a). We could have improved this by better-informing participants of the types of questions we would be asking, especially those which may be sensitive and upsetting. Co-researcher Katy reflected that if disabled young people have seldom been asked such questions, they likely came as a surprise, with the interview context offering little chance to gather and express their thoughts. For example, Christie commented, '... the questions were absolutely fine. [But] I really had to think about my answers as I've never really thought about them before'. Despite this, we found that young people had lots to say: they were forthcoming in speaking about the risks and threats to their lives and bodies, how they mediated 'future' while living shorter lifespans, their excitement for life and living, the ways in which they often grieved for themselves and others and the means through which they were striving to leave something of value to the world. In the remainder of this chapter, we articulate these powerful stories of desiring life while living with death.

THINKING THROUGH OUR KEY FINDINGS: DESIRING LIFE AND LIVING WITH DEATH

Surviving and Thriving

Something unique to this project and to almost all of the young people we spoke to was the desire to really live life in the face of, in spite of, and because of, the very real threat of death. We found that young people had both pragmatism and a desire to live life to the *fullest*, despite their shortened life expectancies:

> Christie: *I always try to do as much as I can while I am still able. An example of this is holidays. I love travelling so I try to go to as many places as I can. There will probably come a time when I'm not fit enough to travel so I'd rather do it now.*

A key finding of the project comes from recognising that many young people living with LL/LTIs are thriving and striving; they have strong desires to live full lives in the present and the future, regardless of how much time they have to live. They truly want to *live*, take risks, make mistakes, experience, learn, love and live fully – but often they do not have the space or freedom to. Disabled young people's ability to live in the present and really enjoy their lives is something that society can learn from, and this ability is apparent in several areas of our research (see Chapter 4). Referring to her children, project participant Ella said:

> *I'm still trying to experience as much as possible but WITH them in*
> *tow so they hopefully will grow up appreciating all life has to offer*
> *as I do. I want to teach them how to truly LIVE!*

It is evident that disabled young people are keen to challenge the notion of disability being a tragedy or that their lives and hopes are in some way reduced. The idea that disabled young people, whose lives are considered and labelled as 'limited', are able to teach others about 'living fully' is a beautiful paradox. This is echoed in disability discourses around Covid-19, where disabled people now find they have a lot to 'teach' the rest of society about what it can mean to live in close proximity to precarity, illness, death and dying, often in isolation, and how to manage this (see Liddiard et al., 2021).

Many young people in our project were creative in their approaches to living and achieving, and were able to articulate their achievements and self-pride in knowing *how* to live in difficult circumstances. Co-researcher Sally reflects on how living with a life-threatening illness has impacted her experiences of time passing and the desire to actively 'live'.

My experience of growing older and approaching birthdays while living with a life-threatening illness reflects the ways I have had to adapt my mindset from that of wider society. There is a conception that as we age we need to attain certain milestones at certain ages. These expectations are sewn into the fabric of our society. There is an expectation, as young people, that after education we will go on to have a career, rent a home, find a partner, buy a house, get married and have a baby. I think one of the reasons people shy away from the joy of growing older is that they feel under pressure to not only reach these milestones but to do so within a certain timeframe. Many disabled young people feel this pressure and strive to feel included. Disability scholar Ellen Samuels (2017, n.p.) explains this longing, saying 'I want to be aligned, synchronous, part of the regular order of the world'. Yet for me, these milestones have become somewhat meaningless. I have reached a place where I no longer measure my life by these predetermined normative chapters. I have adapted both my way of thinking and consequently my way of living to fit my disabled body. Without realising it, I have embraced 'Crip time', where the 'clock bends to meet disabled bodies and minds' (Kafer, 2013, p. 27). I was never able to complete university and required 24 hour care before I could ever graduate. My ill health has meant that for a long time my full-time job turned into trying to stay alive, and this required huge effort and emotional labour (Hochschild, 1983; see Chapter 7). I felt resigned to the fact that I would never accomplish any of these milestones at all. I have had to adapt my attitude and perspective on life. As Samuels (2017, n.p.) describes, I now live my life with a 'flexible approach to normative time frames'. Consequently, I have learned a different way to live, a way that acknowledges the fragility of life and the looming presence of death all the while still loving and living in the here and now.

Even the 'failure' to meet expected milestones has not rid me of the joy of celebrating living another year longer. My life is measured by different milestones. The point of reaching diagnosis, of getting appropriate care in place and more significantly accepting my disability and what it means. Each birthday is a celebration of another year where I have fought to be heard, fought to be provided the correct treatment and fought to keep my body ticking over into a new year. Ultimately it is a celebration of still being alive. This is cause for celebration indeed.

As with the other disabled young people we interviewed who don't know what the future holds, I have to live my life in the present and value each moment. Yet, unsurprisingly, discussing the fragility of their lives was sometimes difficult for disabled young people and many had complicated feelings about the future, living in the present and negotiating death, dying and legacy. They weren't always explicit when talking about death and dying, often death and dying was alluded to through discussion of illness progression and the future, which is where we now turn.

Illness, Threat and Progression

The fear of illness was an ever present threat in the lives of lots of the disabled young people in our project. Many described the feeling of dread at times when they were most likely to become ill. There is a very real awareness that each acute illness could be fatal. Project participant Olivia states:

> *Every time I get a cold it leads to a chest infection. For me this is very serious & often results in pneumonia/pneumothorax/pleurisy & a lengthy hospital admission. I DREAD the winter & all the viruses circulating throughout the community. Each time I get ill, I genuinely fear that it could prove fatal since my respiratory function is in decline.*

Ella describes how the presence of illness, which she has seen friends die from, is one of the most frightening aspects of living with a LL/LTI:

I mostly think about it [her disability being life-limiting] when I'm ill with a chest infection; having difficulty breathing is frightening and I know one of the main causes of death for my type of MD [Muscular Dystrophy] is respiratory failure. I've lost many friends with MD to what started out as just a cold.

For most people, catching a cold is routine, minor and an 'everyday' seasonal illness, but for many disabled young people living with LL/LTIs such eventualities can have gravely serious impacts. Thus, both illness and the progression of impairment were largely conceptualised by young people in our project as *threat and jeopardy.* Christie said:

In the last 8 months I've had many infections which have been very difficult to overcome and the recovery has been quite long because of my disability. Since these recurrent infections, I have become a lot more aware of how my disability can impact my life in other ways and make recovery from infections etc. more complicated.

Critically, it can be seen that illness impacts a young person's sense of self, both in the present and future. It is a precarious time of pain and, for some, leads to reflection upon the future as something that may possibly be denied. Illness and progression often brings a 'loss' – of independence, wellness, and stability – and accordingly this is accompanied by fear. In turn, another burden of emotional labour is incurred when disabled young people process these losses, and they require space and acknowledgement to grieve. Grief is something that disabled young people can experience early in their lives and are often unsupported in, as we discuss later in this chapter.

For those living with LL/LTIs there is clearly a lot of emotional work that goes into finding the balance of living life whilst managing the proximity of death. Medical professionals are only now processing the idea of death in their lives. In a review Co-researcher Sally wrote on the project blog (Whitney, 2018) about 'We need to talk about death', a BBC documentary on palliative care and death, she reflects:

The comprehension [by the medical world] that dying is a part of a person's life, a life that holds journeys, histories and relationships, and is not just a biological event happening to a biological organism, is a breakthrough. It's about recognising the individual as a multi-layered person, giving choice to that person and giving them back the control over their life and their body – ultimately, treating them as a whole. The doctors in the documentary described this shift and change of focus as a tool that 'empowers the patient … [looking] at what's important; the quality as well as the quantity of their lives. It's about not letting disease control your life. It can be seen that medical professionals ultimately reach the same conclusions that disabled young people have already incorporated into their everyday living that, regardless of the length of life or the timescale one has before it ends, each life can be lived to the full, fully completed and that every moment of that life is important no matter its duration. The understanding that the dying process is not just a biological stage nor a failure on behalf of both patient and doctor to 'overcome' a disease was summarised by one of the hospice doctors when he said, 'Dying isn't about dying from a disease, it's about dying from a life'. It was this emphasis on life that was the central theme of the documentary but also our project.

Life Expectancies, Future and Planning

Another key finding was that, often, disabled young people had to wrestle with the pronouncement of life expectancies set by medical professionals and that, for some, managing this could involve significant emotional labour. For example, some young people told us that they doubted health professionals' perspectives about life expectancy and that the 'goal posts' that they had been given about life expectancy were often moved by health professionals as they aged. For some young people, this meant living in a 'liminal' space where they had little knowledge of how long their lives would be. Olivia, described the challenges that this involves:

> *I have come to terms with the fact that my disability will inevitably impact how long I live. Although people with the same condition as me are now living longer due to various treatments and medical intervention, life expectancy is much shorter than the average person. If I live to be 40, I will be happy! But of course, I hope and pray that I will outlive all expectations.*

It could be argued that to counter the forms of emotional work (Liddiard, 2014) and difficulty of living in this 'liminal space' Olivia has set out her own life expectancy. This could be seen as a coping mechanism but it may also be argued that she is embracing the reality of her situation. Whichever it may be, it is clear that she maintains hope that she will live longer and this is another important finding of the project – disabled young people *desire* life. As interviewee Ella states:

> *I'm a cup half full person. Trying to remain positive and to find the positive in any given situation. How do I feel about it [her disability] being life-limiting? Well, I haven't ever known any different so this is normal to me, so looking at it positively, I guess never knowing any different makes it easier for me to just get on with it.*

Similarly, Christie describes the desire to get on with the process of living: 'If I'm honest, I have never asked or researched how long I am likely to live. I've never really wanted to know'. Ramesh, another participant, was very clear in how he felt about life expectancy, his life being limited and what 'living' is really about:

> *[...] a life-limiting condition has a significant impact on your life … I think it's about quality of life rather than length of life, that's the most important thing, I mean you could live 100 years but be miserable.*

However, it is clear that living with a LL/LTI does affect decisions and plans for the future that disabled young people make. There was a consciousness of wanting to 'cram' life in, to make the most of life especially as impairment progresses. One participant, Ella, states, 'This year I've tried to cram more goals in because I feel myself getting worse. So we've got a few trips planned'.

Disabled young people discussed how, in living with the reality of a LL/LTI (both in terms of life span and the health challenges involved), they have had to pick and choose what goals are most important to them and that their 'chosen' goals (and their ability and decision to follow them) may not reflect normative aspirations. Olivia says:

> *I had a particularly bad bout of pneumonia in 2013. It took many months for me to recover & was incredibly difficult to overcome both physically & mentally. At that point, my priorities changed. Up until then I had been pushing (& struggling!) to move out of my parental home, and to find employment. So, realising how fragile my body is, I decided to stop the aimless search for accommodation. To this day, I still live with my parents in their home. It's far from ideal but the process had been going on for almost 2 years & was very stressful, with no end in sight.*

Many participants also acknowledged the need to be flexible in making plans for the future due to changing health needs, but also the impact this has on their feelings about themselves and the emotional labour involved in maintaining positive wellbeing. Sam states:

> I think it's important to set goals but be flexible. Health and other life circumstances can change what you can and cannot manage, and sometimes goals set in stone that you can no longer achieve only make you feel bad about yourself.

For some, this eventuality (the prospect of a shortened life) impacted upon life planning, particularly in terms of having a family (see Chapter 6). One young person, Ella, describes how she decided to have children, despite being told this wasn't possible according to doctors. She describes her zest to get on with living despite the opinions of others. Ella comments:

> [...] people may ... judge me for carrying on with my life, having children knowing it's likely I won't see them get married, have kids, etc. ... [but] hopefully [they] will grow up appreciating all life has to offer as I do.

Ella explains how this has affected the way she now lives her life and her conscious consideration between 'cramming in life' against the after-effects of an activity. She describes how before having children:

> I used to just go for any type of experience just to experience it and not think about how many days of recovery I'd need after. Now I have to weigh up if certain things are worth the aftermath for my kids' sake. Though at the same time, I'm still trying to experience as much as possible but WITH them in tow .... But yes, I pick more wisely.

However, for another disabled young woman, Olivia, a period of severe illness has had far-reaching implications for both her present and her future, particularly the decision to find a romantic partner and have children, despite going against her deepest desires for her life and bringing the reality of dying earlier into plain sight. Olivia comments:

> Because I am so aware of the seriousness of my condition & the fact it is life-limiting, I am reluctant to enter into romantic relationships. I don't think it's fair on the other person. Some years before that I came to terms with the fact that I wouldn't be able to have children. This was major for me as this is the only thing I have ever REALLY wanted from life.

The notion of romantic involvement not being '"fair on the other person' could be seen as a good example of the extent to which internalised ableism impacts disabled young people's sexual and intimate selves and futures (Liddiard, 2018a; see Chapter 6). But it's clear that the context of a short life exacerbates these worries even further.

Disabled young people routinely discussed how their plans for the future were also shaped both by their health, impairments and the expectations of others around them. One participant, Sam, has noticed a marked difference in the expectations others have for their life after becoming disabled, compared to their life prior to acquiring disability. Sam says:

> *I feel like sometimes my ambitions aren't respected as much now as when I was 'able bodied' [sic] as they're not as lofty, they have less of an impact.*

Another participant, Anna, describes how her educational aspirations were downplayed and not encouraged. She states, 'Dad might say about my education: "As long as you are enjoying your course" … rather than trying to push me forward to achieve even greater levels'. While Hunter acknowledges that his future planning holds a lot of unknowns due to the disabling barriers of society and lack of care support, yet this doesn't hold him back:

> *I am applying for jobs at the moment but I don't know how anything is going to work yet … and I don't know if it will work or how it will work … but I have applied for them anyway.*

When probed further about the support that he needs to accomplish this goal, Hunter describes a determination to forge ahead that is reflective of the determination and striving of many of the disabled young people we interviewed. However, he does describe how his care is a limiting factor and acknowledges the labour required to get the support he needs:

> *I will cross that bridge [getting the right support] when I come to it, but at the moment I am actually struggling with [care] hours, we are going back and forth with the social worker and they do not seem to be giving me anymore hours yet, so we are going to go back to them … but it might be a problem, but I'll think of something I can get around, through campaigning and support and stuff like that.*

Notably, this was something that we noticed disabled young people often routinely lack the space to live their own lives in their own ways and to have these acknowledged and be given appropriate support. For example, Ella said explicitly that the 'only thing that'll stop me [achieving her goals] is me getting ill/going into hospital or not having the right PAs to support these activities I've planned'. In the same way, Christie describes how her ability to carry out plans and live more expansively are limited, saying:

Health and lack of accessibility are both the reasons for this .... Lack of accessibility is another big issue and often I miss out on going to gigs because the venue doesn't have wheelchair access or the lift is broken. I've lost count of the number of times this has happened.

The awareness of the fragility of life and their bodies means that disabled young people tend to live their lives now, in the present, with visceral intimacy with their bodies. Olivia says ' ... my primary focus now is health & happiness. I have to do what is best to protect & care for my body'.

Co-researcher Sally describes a similar mentality: I have felt the need to embrace the present and the reality I find myself in. More than that, I feel compelled to actively demarcate the positives in my life and triumph in *knowing* how to live in often difficult circumstances. My grandfather and I decided in my twenties that if I had not graduated from university by the time I was 30 then we would have another form of graduation ceremony, a ceremony where we celebrated that I had navigated the hurdles and weathered the storms of remaining alive despite life-threatening conditions. His acknowledgement of the fact that I was still maturing as an individual in the face of adversity was just as significant, if not more, as graduating from university and following a career. I felt that he understood my need to celebrate my own vitality.

Living with Grief

In this section, Co-researcher Katy reflects upon her experiences of grief being a part of youth and friendship. Katy's words below are reflective of the many stories of living with grief told by our young participants. The normalisation of death, the ignorance towards disabled young people's grief, and living with losing others as routine were often key experiences for our participants living with LL/LTIs:

By the time I was 25 years old, I had been to eight funerals and none of those people were older than me. I have grown up with a close circle of disabled friends and death has been a large part of our collective experience, but this was largely overlooked by those around us. From a young age, I remember being called into a sudden assembly to be told a child had died, there would be a minute's silence, then we were encouraged to go back to the classroom and the child was rarely mentioned again. Attending a special school meant these assemblies were unfortunately not a rare occurrence. It has always irked me that when a death occurs in a mainstream school the news often reports that students are receiving professional support, yet we were given nothing. Death felt like an accepted part of life for us and the staff didn't seem able to handle our feelings, so shut them down. This relates to Runswick-Cole's (2010) observation that when death features disability it is viewed differently to non-disabled young people as it is seen as a release from suffering. Although in part this may be true and, for some, death is welcomed rather than feared, the heightened focus on a 'release from suffering' plays into the ableist construct of tragedy.

I was 18 when one of my best friends died. Death played a bigger role in my life from then on as my friends' conditions worsened and the realisation of what that meant set in. Many friends didn't feel able to talk to their families about dying for fear of upsetting them, so friends became their sounding board. I think the level of depth to these conversations made us much closer and led us to place a higher value on our time together than I think we would have otherwise. The shared experience of dying, death and grief has created a unique collective within which we have traditions to remember friends and a deep understanding of each other's experiences, as well as a drive to live our lives to the fullest and make memories.

When I step back I know this experience is very different to my non-disabled peers. Whilst doing my exams at university a friend died and I told my lecturer. However, when another friend died a few days later I didn't feel able to say, because it felt too far removed from the experience of my peers to such an extent that I feared not being believed.

I carry some guilt that my condition does not necessarily shorten my life and I will outlive many of my friends. When grief is raw there is always anger about the time of which my friend has been robbed. I think living with the knowledge that some lives are shorter is a major element in my friendship circle and I feel immensely lucky to be surrounded by people who don't shy away from the difficult aspects of life. Whilst I would much rather have the opportunity to grow old with my friends it has created a force within us all where we appreciate every minute together, and living life to the full becomes the foundation of our friendship, and what unites us.

Grief comes in many forms and does not necessarily always mean death. When participants were asked what the term 'life limiting' meant to them, some assigned it to the medical context of shortened lives, but a substantial number also referred to the ways their lives are limited or restricted due to disabling factors. Greg states:

If I can't do things because of my disability, I can't be a part of society, or do normal things that other people do because of my disability, I would say that is life limiting as well.

Anna adds:

Life-limiting means to me that it prevents you from having a choice in living your life in the way you want to. This could mean that whenever you want to go somewhere away from your familiar home environment you need to take extra equipment with you – a ventilator maybe, or a coughing machine or a mobile hoist or a commode, the list is endless

Olivia expressed grief for how she feels like she is missing out: 'I miss out due to health problems & accessibility issues. Soooo many times I have made plans & have then had to cancel due to illness'.

It has become common within British culture to silence the experience of dying and grief. Clearly, disabled young people have far more emotional literacy in this area than they are given credit for. In fact, the experiences we have highlighted in this chapter so far show that there is a possibility disabled young people are more able to *be* with these aspects of life than the adults surrounding them.

LEAVING LEGACIES

In this final section, we contemplate legacy. Legacy is a meaningful and multifaceted way in which information, values and possessions are passed on to others. It can also be a way to be remembered and memorialised by loved ones, allies and communities. We want to state here that the disabled young people in our project chose to build legacies in very different ways, and that no one way is any more important than another – all legacies have value. We follow Mia Mingus (2010a, n.p.), who politicises *evidence* as a central part of legacy:

We must leave evidence. Evidence that we were here, that we existed, that we survived and loved and ached. Evidence of the wholeness we never felt and the immense sense of fullness we gave to each other. Evidence of who we were, who we thought we were, who we never should have been. Evidence for each other that there are other ways to live-past survival; past isolation.

In this conclusion, then, we first contemplate what legacy means for the disabled young people at the centre of our project; we also attend to the nuances in different types of legacy building in which participants were often routinely engaged. In the second part of this conclusion, we consider the legacies of our project – The Living Life to the Fullest Project. We contemplate the legacies of the knowledge both it, and we, have produced; the way in which the stories we have retold in this book can serve as evidence of and solidarity with other disabled young people living with LL/LTIs. We also explore the project's legacy in bringing changes to research, inquiry and academia; and finally, we emphasise that our key legacy is encouraging others to value disability and difference.

What Legacy Means for the Disabled Young People at the Centre of Our Project

An acknowledgement by others, both in the present but also in the future, and after death, was something of deep importance to disabled young people across our project, the latter being defined as 'legacy'. The idea of legacy took on different shapes and meanings for different people. We found that 'leaving a legacy' was nuanced – our young participants centred on intimate legacies, digital legacies, activist legacies and their own blogging, writing and leaving evidence as key forms of legacy building. In this section, we list and explain these:

Intimate legacies: Many of the disabled young people we interviewed were aware of leaving a legacy by being remembered by those important to them. Olivia said:

> *I often say, I hope to live long enough to see [my nephew] grow up. I want most of all for him to remember me! So this is my biggest goal .*

Ella declared 'I want [my children] to remember me very much present in their daily lives'.

Digital legacies: Many young people talked readily about their digital legacies. By this, we are referring primarily to the meanings of digital spaces, technologies and worlds for end of life, death and dying. Participants talked about building and leaving legacies on their blogs, vlogs and social media accounts. As more and more of our lives move into digital worlds we are leaving an online footprint of our lives, selves and relationships with others in and across multiple communities (Bellamy et al., 2013). According to Gulotta et al. (2013, p. 1813):

*as digital systems and information become meaningfully parts of
people's everyday and social relationships, it is essential to develop
new insights about how technology intersects with legacy and
inheritance practices.*

It is estimated that:

*by the end of the century, depending on Facebook's user growth
rate, the dead profiles are even expected to exceed the number of
living user profiles, thereby creating a form of 'digital graveyard'.
(Öhman and Floridi, 2017, p. 639)*

Yet, digital legacies do far more than group and distribute our digital assets to
loved ones after we die. Digital worlds offer the means to construct identity,
in life and death:

*interactive systems provide objects and collections through which
people construct and express aspects of their identity. Increasingly,
this personal content is kept online, in the form of social network
accounts, game systems, personal websites, and photo collections,
all internet-based resources that people draw on to explore,
establish, and express aspects of their identity. (Gulotta et al., 2013,
p. 1814)*

Thus, digital legacy building can offer self-managed ways through which to
actively construct our memory to others, as well as the story of our lives and
selves. For example, Co-researcher Lucy, who led us into the concept of digital
legacy through her own experiences, has blogged (Watts, 2017, n.p.):

*I spend much of my life online, naturally using social media sites
including Facebook, Twitter, YouTube and Google+, Instagram
and Linkedin. I have a life-limiting condition, meaning I have had
to do my end of life planning and put things in place for when the
time comes, including my advanced care plan, my funeral wishes
and lasting power of attorney (LPA). Naturally, my social media
will is a part of that end of life planning. I have kept putting this
off but have finally completed my social media will and will give
a copy to my family and keep a copy in my files. We live so much
of our lives online. However, we are all going to die one day. What
happens to our social media accounts when that happens? Well,
unless we plan for it, the account could be left online when we
don't want it to be, or it could be deleted against our wishes by
well meaning family members. It's important we all plan ahead for*

our deaths, including our social media will. You may want your account to be memorialised, closed or deactivated. You may want it to be kept online for people to remember you by and to interact with your account, much like visiting your grave but online instead. However you may want your social media accounts closed and your information taken off the internet. Having my social media will means my mum knows exactly what I want to happen to my account. She will also post blogs for me after I have died and upload the legacy video I have just made. Not only will she be left with the social media will, but I have created a document with instructions on how to manage my accounts, how to post blogs and how to share the legacy video, so that she can follow my wishes exactly.

Moreover, Lucy emphasises the Digital Legacy Association's Social Media Will, which can allow you to fill out all your account details for nominated people to receive after your death, to support the maintenance of your digital legacy. However, Lucy's work extends to thinking about the digitalisation of her death and funeral (Watts, 2018, n.p.):

I'm planning a series of blogs for my mother to post after my death on my blog, Lucy's Light, and also some social media posts too. I'm creating a legacy film, a form of documentary of me for my family to hear me and see me and listen to me talking about myself, my life, any advice and so on, but this will also be uploaded to YouTube and posted on my blog so that if people stumble on my work after my death, they can get to know me through this film. For this, I am creating video tutorials to enable my mother to carry out my wishes to post the blogs and upload the video. I am also looking into my funeral being live-streamed to Facebook so my friends unable to attend physically can participate. This allows me some control over how I am remembered after my death and brings me some comfort.

Activist legacies: Taking action in the present with the intention of affecting changes, often for others, that carry forward into the future beyond their own life span, is a crucial way some disabled young people create legacies. For project participants Helen and Josh, they use their time and energy on educating the services around them with which they have had personal experiences to improve understanding of the lives of disabled people. They explain: 'We are doing a lot of work with NHS England around personalised care and trying to implement that on a wider scale'. Helen and Josh are using Personal Health Budgets for the benefit of other disabled people, as this is something that they have had to fight for themselves. As a couple, described in Chapter 6, they have also worked hard to combat difficulties and assumptions about their sexuality and worked to create ways to have an active sex life. In this too, they aspire to make changes that benefit everyone both now and in the future:

what we would really like is [for disabled people] to be able to see an occupational therapist [with the] NHS to be able to talk about how you have been feeling, your sex life, because we feel that is an important part of life.

However, Helen shares their concerns that the legacies that she and Josh leave behind are for causes they believe in:

'We want to use our disability to affect change and we want to use opportunities; so whenever somebody asks us', 'will you do this media thing?' – we want to investigate it, we ask a lot of questions first, what's the story that you are trying to portray? Is it, 'oh these people have got a disability and they have got married – it's amazing!' – If that's the story then we are like 'no'. If the story is how getting a PHB [personal health budgets] enabled us to get married and if we had more PHBs then more people could do the same, then we are like 'yeah, yeah we definitely want to support that message'.

Interestingly, the couple centre faith within their activism and advocacy work. Powerfully, Helen recognises that she has influence, both now and in the future, and through her faith and finding her identity in God; she has a drive to

stand up for people who are more vulnerable than me and be a voice for people who don't necessarily have a voice and to use my life to make a difference.

She describes the nature of her own empowerment:

God has enabled us to make things better for other people and we are empowered to have an effect on the world, because we are powerful and effective people, not that we are disabled.

Autobiographical legacies: The need to have one's voice heard (and accurately portrayed) is a common factor amongst many of our project participants. Jude describes leaving a physical legacy in the form of a book: 'I have written a book through voice recognition technology … and again that is portraying my voice and making sure we are not forgotten'. It can be seen again how vital it is to disabled young people with LL/LTIs to be remembered. We note that this follows the life writing efforts from within disabled people's movements.

We are also proud of the legacies of our project and our book:

Legacies around knowledge production: We want to emphasise the importance of disabled people carrying out research about their own lives, as we have done throughout this book. As Ignagni et al. (2016, p. 132) state, 'knowledge produced about disability life rarely includes labelled [disabled] people as competent commentators on their own life conditions'. Thus, it is vital to disseminate the rare and rich knowledges of disability produced through this project and book to others: families, disability communities and education, health and social care professionals.

Crip-solidarity legacies: We hope the book's legacy will provide comfort to disabled young people who see lives similar to their own being represented which has seldom happened to date. All co-researchers have experienced various forms of isolation and have a strong desire to reach out to others in this position. Therefore, the crip-solidarity created through this project is an important legacy to us. For us personally, it has built friendships and allowed us to find a safe space to explore difficult aspects of our own lives. Academically, the collision of personal experience, passions and theoretical knowledge have enabled us to identify gaps in research and see opportunities for future research, meaning the legacy of this book could be the springboard for creating other important legacies in the future.

Ableism legacies: Challenging ableism is a key legacy of this project through participants' stories, our personal reflections and the research approaches used. We have highlighted the various ways ableism happens in disabled young people's lives, from assumptions about their sexuality to the extra emotional labour undertaken when living in an ableist world. By documenting this throughout the book we hope to raise awareness of how ableism and disablism routinely impact the lives of disabled young people.

Legacies for research: Lastly, we want to emphasise the legacies we hope this project has made for inquiry and research contexts. The Living Life to the Fullest Project has shown that disabled young people can be, and should be, research leaders in research about their own lives, making decisions, engaging and co-leading across the process and being centred in the collection, analysis and writing up of data (see Chapter 3).

CONCLUSION

Finally, we want to end our book by emphasising the importance of valuing disability. We hope we've shown that disability is a rich and undeniably human experience. The young people across our project have stressed the fullness of their lives, and they've done so in ableist and disablist cultures that deny them access, personhood and render their lives unliveable. We've shown that disability can be beautifully disruptive; it can change the ways we think about and understand life, death, faith, work, care, sex, art, activism, community and love. This is where we want to leave our reader, with an understanding that disability is valued, valuable, rich and full.

REFERENCES

Abbott, D. and Carpenter, J. 2014. 'Wasting precious time': young men with Duchenne muscular dystrophy negotiate the transition to adulthood, *Disability & Society*, 29(8), 1192–1205.

Abbott, D., Carpenter, J., Gibson, B.E., Hastie, J., Jepson, M. and Smith, B. 2019. Disabled men with muscular dystrophy negotiate gender, *Disability and Society*, 34(5), 683–703.

Abbott, D. and Howarth, J. 2007. Still off-limits? Staff views on supporting gay, lesbian and bisexual people with intellectual disabilities to develop sexual and intimate relationships?, *Journal of Applied Research in Intellectual Disabilities*, 20(2), 116–126.

Abell, S., Ashmore, J., Beart, S., Brownley, P., Butcher, A., Clarke, Z., Combes, H., Francis, E., Hayes, S., Hem-mingham, I., Hicks, K., Ibraham, A., Kenyon, E., Lee, D., McClimens, A., Collins, M., Newton, J. and Wilson, D. 2007. Including everyone in research: the Burton Street Group, *British Journal of Learning Disabilities*, 35(2), 121–124.

Ahmed, S. 2004. *The Cultural Politics of Emotion*, New York, NY, Routledge.

Ahmed, S. 2010. Killing joy: feminism and the history of happiness, *Signs*, 35(3), 571–594.

Andrews, E.E. and Ayers, K. 2016. Parenting with disability: experiences of disabled women. In *Eliminating Inequities for Women with Disabilities: An Agenda for Health and Wellness*, Eds S.E. Miles-Cohen and C. Signore, pp. 209–225, Washington, DC, American Psychological Association. https://doi.org/10.1037/14943-011

Bailey, S., Boddy, K., Briscoe, S. and Morris, C. 2014. Involving disabled children and young people as partners in research: a systematic review, *Child: Care, Health and Development*, 41, 505–514.

Barnes, C. 1992. *Disabling Imagery and the Media: An Exploration of the Principles for Media Representations of Disabled People*, Halifax: The British Council of Organisations of Disabled People and Ryburn Publishing Ltd.

Bartky, S.L. 1990. *Femininity and Domination: Studies in the Phenomenology of Oppression*, New York, NY, Routledge.

Barton, L. and Clough, P. Eds 1998. *Articulating with Difficulty: Research Voices in Special Education*, London, Paul Chapman Ltd.

Barton, L. and Oliver, M. 1997. *Disability Studies: Past Present and Future*, Leeds, The Disability Press.

Bates, K., Goodley, D. and Runswick-Cole, K. 2017. Precarious lives and resistant possibilities: the labour of people with learning disabilities in times of austerity, *Disability & Society*, 32(2), 160–175. doi:10.1080/09687599.2017.1281105

Bellamy, C.J., Arnold, M.V., Gibbs, M.R., Nansen, B. and Kohn, T. 2013. *Death and the Internet: Consumer Issues for Planning and Managing Digital Legacies*, Sydney, Australian Communications Consumer Action Network. Available at: http://accan.org.au/files/death_and_the_internet.pdf

Bennett, L. and Segerberg, A. 2011. Digital media and the personalization of collective action: social technology and the organization of protest against the global economic crisis, *Information, Communication and Society*, 14, 770–799.

Beresford, B. 2012. Working on well-being: researchers' experiences of a participative approach to understanding the subjective well-being of disabled young people, *Children & Society*, 26, 234–240.

Beresford, P. 2004. Madness, distress, research and a social model. In *Implementing the Social Model of Disability: Theory and Research*, Eds C. Barnes and G. Mercer, pp. 208–222, Leeds, The Disability Press.

Bloom, B.S. 1956. *Taxonomy of Educational Objectives, Handbook: The Cognitive Domain*, New York, NY, David McKay.

Bowker, N. and Tuffin, K. 2004. Using the online medium for discursive research about people with disabilities, *Social Science Computer Review*, 22(2), 228–241.

Braidotti, R. 2013. *The Posthuman*, London, Polity.

Braidotti, R. 2019. A theoretical framework for the critical posthumanities, *Theory, Culture & Society*, 36(6), 31–61.

Braidotti, R. and Regan, L. 2017. Our times are always out of joint: feminist relational ethics in and of the world today: an interview with Rosi Braidotti, *Women: A Cultural Review*, 28(3), 171–192.

Brothers, E. 2020. Building back better – disabled people and COVID-19, Community, 3rd December 2020 [Online]. Available at: https://community-tu.org/building-back-better-disabled-people-and-covid-19/#a10287c4 [Accessed 2 February 2021].

Bucknall, S. 2010. Children as researchers in English primary schools: developing a model for good practice. Paper presented at the British Educational Research Association Annual Conference, University of Warwick, 1–4 September 2010.

Burch, L. 2016. Tackling disability discrimination and disability hate crime: a multidisciplinary guide, *Disability & Society*, 31(10), 1408–1409.

Burch, L. 2021. *Understanding Disability and Everyday Hate*, Cham, Palgrave Macmillan.

Byrne, B. and Kelly, B. 2015. Special issue: Valuing disabled children: participation and inclusion, *Child Care in Practice*, 21, 197–200.

Carr, D. 2010. Constructing disability in online worlds: conceptualising disability in online research, *London Review of Education*, 8, 51–61.

Carter, B. and Coyne, I. 2018. Participatory research: does it genuinely extend the sphere of children's and young people's participation? In *Being Participatory: Researching with Children and Young People*, Eds I. Coyne and B. Carter, pp. 171–178, London, Springer.

Chappell, L., Goodley, D. and Lawthom, R. 2002. Making connections: the relevances of the social model of disability for people with learning difficulties, *British Journal of Learning Disabilities*, 29(2), 45–50.

Chapple, A., Ziebland, S. and Hawton, K. 2015. Taboo and the different death? Perceptions of those bereaved by suicide or other traumatic death, *Sociology of Health & Illness*, 37(4), 610–625.

Chataika, T. 2012. Postcolonialism, disability and development. In *Social Theories of Disability: New Developments and Directions*, Eds D. Goodley and B. Hughes, pp. 252–269, London, Routledge.

Children Act 2004, c. 31. Available at: http://www.legislation.gov.uk/ukpga/2004/31/contents [Accessed 17 September 2021].

Claassens, J. 2012. Ruth, Tamar and the quest for human dignity, *The Catholic Biblical Quarterly*, 74(4), 659–674.

Claassens, J., Shaikh, S. and Swartz, L. 2018. Engaging disability and religion in the Global South. In *The Palgrave Handbook of Disability and Citizenship in the Global South*, Eds B. Watermayer, J. McKenzie and L. Swartz, pp. 147–164, Cham, Palgrave Macmillan.

Clarke, S. and Holdsworth, L. 2017. Flexibility in the workplace: implications for flexible work arrangements for individuals, teams and organisations [Online]. Available at: https://www.bl.uk/collect ion-items/acasc-flexibility-in-the-workplace-2017# [Accessed 20 May 2021].

Clavering, E.K. and McLaughlin, J. 2010. Children's participation in health research: from objects to agents?. *Child: Care, Health and Development*, 36, 603–611.

Coad, J. and Lewis, A. 2004. Engaging children and young people in research: literature review for the national evaluation of the children's fund [Online]. Available at: http://www.necf.org/core_files/ Elicitingchdrnsviewsjanecoadannlewisoct2004.doc [Accessed 21 May 2018].

Coates, W.H. and White, H.V. 1970. *The Ordeal of Liberal Humanism: An Intellectual History of Western Europe*, New York, NY, McGraw-Hill.

Crow, L. 1996. Including all of our lives. In *Encounters with Strangers: Feminism and Disability*, Ed. J. Morris, pp. 206–226, London, The Women's Press.

Curran, T. and Runswick-Cole, K. 2013. *Disabled Children's Childhood Studies: Critical Approaches in a Global Context*, Basingstoke, Palgrave MacMillan.

Curran, T. and Runswick-Cole, K. 2014. Disabled children's childhood studies: an emerging domain of inquiry?. *Disability & Society*, 29, 1617–1630.

Davis, L.J. 2010. *The Disability Studies Reader*, 3rd ed., New York, NY, Routledge.

De Graeve, K. 2010. The limits of intimate citizenship: reproduction of difference in Flemish-Ethiopian 'adoption cultures', *Bioethics*, 24(4), 365–372.

Delio, I. 2011. *Compassion: Living in the Spirit of St. Francis*, Cincinnati, OH, St Anthony Messenger Press.

DfES (Department for Education and Skills). 2003. *Every Child Matters. Green Paper, Cm. 5860*, London, The Stationery Office (TSO).

Dinwoodie, R., Greenhill, B. and Cookson, A. 2020. Them two things are what collide together': understanding the sexual identity experiences of lesbian, gay, bisexual and trans people labelled with intellectual disability, *Journal of Applied Research in Intellectual Disabilities*, 33(1), 3–16.

Disabilities and Faith. 2016. Training faith-based organizations on how to be more welcoming and accessible [Online]. Available at: http://www. disabilitiesandfaith.org/ [Accessed 30 September 2017].

Draucker, C.B., Martsolf, D.S. and Poole, C. 2009. Developing distress protocols for research on sensitive topics, *Archives of Psychiatric Nursing*, 23(5), 343–350.

Durose, C., Beebeejaun, Y., Rees, J., Richardson, J. and Richardson, L. 2012. *Towards Coproduction in Research with Communities*, Swindon, AHRC.

Earle, S. 1999. Facilitated sex and the concept of sexual need: disabled students and their personal assistants, *Disability & Society*, 14(3), 309–323.

EHRC. 2016. Being disabled in Britain 2016: a journey less equal [Online]. Available at: https://www.equalityhumanrights.com/sites/default/files/being-disabled-in-britain.pdf [Accessed on 15 October 2018].

Eisland, N.L. 1994. *The Disabled God: Toward a Liberatory Theology of Disability*, Nashville, TN, Abingdon Press.

Ellis, K., Garland-Thomson, R., Kent, M. and Robertson, R. 2018. *Manifestos for the Future of Critical Disability Studies*, London, Routledge.

Engelsrud, G. 2005. The lived body as experience and perspective: methodological challenges, *Qualitative Research*, 5, 267–284.

Eysenbach, G. 2001. Ethical issues in qualitative research on internet communities, *British Medical Journal*, 323, 1103–1105.

Fargas-Malet, M., McSherry, D., Larkin, E. and Robinson, C. 2010. Research with children: methodological issues and innovative techniques, *Journal of Early Childhood Research*, 8(2), 175–192.

Frank, A. 2016. Vocational rehabilitation: supporting ill or disabled individuals in (to) work: a UK perspective, *Healthcare*, 4(3), 46. https://doi.org/10.3390/healthcare4030046

Fudge, N., Wolfe, C.D.A. and McKevitt, C. 2007. Involving older people in health research, *Age and Ageing*, 36, 492–500.

Gibson, B.E., Mistry, B., Smith, B., Yoshida, K.K., Abbott, D., Lindsay, S. and Hamdani, Y. 2014. Becoming men: gender, disability, and transitioning to adulthood, *Health*, 18, 95–114.

Gilroy, P. 2018. Where every breeze speaks of courage and liberty: offshore humanism and marine xenology, or, racism and the problem of critique at sea level. *Antipode*, 5, 3–22.

Goggin, G. and Newell, C. 2003. *Digital Disability: The Social Construction of Disability in New Media*, Lanham, MD, Rowman & Littlefield.

Goggin, G. and Newell, C. 2007. The business of digital disability, *The Information Society*, 24(2), 159–168.

Golden, J. 1996. Critical imagination: serious play with narrative and gender, *Gender and Education*, 8(3), 323–336.

Goodley, D. 2011. *Disability Studies: An Interdisciplinary Introduction*, London, Sage.

Goodley, D. 2012. Dis/entangling critical disability studies, *Disability & Society*, 27(6), 631–644.

Goodley, D. 2014. *Dis/ability Studies. Theorising Disablism and Ableism*, London, Routledge.

Goodley, D. 2016. *Disability Studies: An Interdisciplinary Introduction*, 2nd ed., London, Sage.

Goodley, D. 2020. *Disability and Other Human Questions*, London, Emerald Publishers Ltd.

Goodley, D., Lawthom, R. and Runswick-Cole, K. 2014a. Dis/ability and austerity: beyond work and slow death, *Disability & Society*, 29(6), 980–984, doi:10.1080/09687599.2014.920125

Goodley, D., Lawthom, R. and Runswick-Cole, K. 2014b. Posthuman disability studies, *Subjectivity*, 7(1), 342–361.

Goodley, D., Lawthom, R., Liddiard, K. and Runswick-Cole, K. 2018a. Posthuman disability and DisHuman studies. In *Posthuman Glossary*, Eds R. Braidotti and M. Hlavajova, pp. 342–345, London, Bloomsbury.

Goodley, D., Lawthom, R., Liddiard, K. and Runswick-Cole, K. 2018b. A dishuman manifesto, by ProjectDisHuman. In *Manifestos for the Future of Critical Disability Studies*, Eds R. Garland-Thompson, M. Kent, K. Ellis and R. Robertson, pp. 179–187, Oxon, Routledge.

Goodley, D., Lawthom, R., Liddiard, K. and Runswick-Cole, K. 2019. Provocations for critical disability studies, *Disability & Society*, 34(6), 972–997.

Goodley, D., Liddiard, K. and Runswick-Cole, K. 2018c. Feeling disability: theories of affect and critical disability studies, *Disability & Society*, 33(2), 197–217.

Goodley, D. and Runswick-Cole, K. 2014. Becoming dis/human: thinking about the human through disability, *Discourse: Studies in the Cultural Politics of Education*, 37(1), 1–15.

Goodley, D., Runswick-Cole, K. and Liddiard, K. 2015. The DisHuman child, *Discourse: The Cultural Politics of Education*, 37, 770–784. https:// doi.org/10.1080/01596306.2015.1075731

Goodley, D. and Tregaskis, C. 2006. Storying disability and impairment: retrospective accounts of disabled family life, *Qualitative Health Research*, 16(5), 630–646.

Googin, G. 2018. Technology and social futures. In *Manifestos for the Future of Critical Disability Studies*, Eds K. Ellis, R. Garland-Thomson, M. Kent and R. Robertson, pp. 79–90, London, Routledge.

Gulotta, R., Odom, W., Forlizzi, J. and Faste, H. 2013. Digital artifacts as legacy: exploring the lifespan and value of digital data. In *Proceedings of the SIGCHI Conference on Human Factors in Computing Systems*, April, pp. 1813–1822, New York, NY, ACM.

Gumbel, N. 2020. *The Bible in One Year – A Commentary*, London, Hodder & Staughton.

Hallett, C. and Prout, A. 2003. *Hearing the Voices of Children: Social Policy for a New Century*, London, Routledge.

Hamraie, A. and Fritsch, K. 2019. Crip technoscience manifesto, *Catalyst: Feminism, Theory, Technoscience*, 5(1), 1–34.

Hewson, C.M. 2014. Research methods on the Internet. In *Communication and Technology*, Eds J.A. Danowski and L. Cantoni, pp. 277–303, Handbooks of Communication Sciences Series, Berlin, De Gruyter Mouton.

Hewson, C.M., Yule, P., Laurent, D. and Vogel, C.M. 2003. *Internet Research Methods: A Practical Guide for the Social and Behavioural Sciences. New Technologies for Social Research*, London, Sage.

Hirst, N. and Foster, D. 2021. Covid is changing the way we work – and for disabled people too [Online]. Available at: https://theconversation.com/ covid-is-changing-the-way-we-work-and-for-disabled-people-too-150670 [Accessed 14 May 2021].

Hochschild, A.R. 1983. *The Managed Heart: Commercialization of Human Feeling*, Berkeley, CA, University of California Press.

Huffaker, D.A. and Calvert, S.L. 2005. Gender, identity, and language use in teenage blogs, *Journal of Computer-Mediated Communication*, 10(2), 1–27.

Hunter, J., Runswick-Cole, K., Goodley, D. and Lawthom, R. 2019. Plans that work, *British Journal of Special Education*, 47(2), 134–151.

Ignagni, E., Fudge-Schormans, A., Liddiard, K. and Runswick-Cole, K. 2016. Some people aren't allowed to love: intimate citizenship in the lives of people labelled with intellectual disabilities, *Disability and Society*, 31(1), 131–135.

Imhoff, S. 2017. Why disability studies needs to take religion seriously, *Religions*, 8(9), 186.

INVOLVE. 2016. *Involving Children and Young People in Research: Top Tips and Essential Key Issues for Researchers*, Eastleigh, INVOLVE.

James, A. and Prout, A. 1997. *Constructing and Reconstructing Childhood*, 2nd ed., Basingstoke, Falmer Press.

Johnson, K. and Walmsley, J. 2010. *Towards a Good Life*, Bristol, Policy Press.

Jong, S.T. 2017. Netnography: researching online populations. In *Handbook of Research Methods in Health Social Sciences*, Ed. P. Liamputtong, pp. 1321–1337, Singapore, Springer.

Kafer, A. 2013. *Feminist Queer Crip*, Bloomington, IN, Indiana University Press.

Kay, E. and Tisdall, M. 2017. Conceptualising children and young people's participation: examining vulnerability, social accountability and co-production, *The International Journal of Human Rights*, 21, 59–75.

Kellett, M. 2005a. Children as active researchers: a new research paradigm for the 21st century? In *ESRC National Centre for Research Methods, NCRM Methods Review Papers*, London, ESRC.

Kellett, M. 2005b. *How to Develop Children as Researchers: A Step-by-Step Guide to Teaching the Research Process*, London, Paul Chapman/Sage.

Kellett, M. 2010. *Rethinking Children and Research: Attitudes in Contemporary Society*, London, Continuum.

Kirby, P. 2004. *A Guide to Actively Involving Young People in Research: For Researchers, Research Commissioners, and Managers*, Eastleigh, INVOLVE.

Kitchin, R. 1998. 'Out of place', 'knowing one's place': space, power and the exclusion of disabled people', *Disability & Society*, 13(3), 343–356.

Kittay, E.F. 2019. *Learning from My Daughter: The Value and Care of Disabled Minds*, New York, NY, Oxford University Press.

Klang, N., Göransson, K., Lindqvist, G., Nilholm, C., Hansson, S. and Bengtsson, K. 2020. Instructional Practices for Pupils with an Intellectual Disability in Mainstream and Special Educational Settings, *International Journal of Disability, Development and Education*, 67(2), 151–166.

Koopman, N. 2012. Hope, vulnerability and disability? A theological perspective In *Searching for Dignity: Conversations on Human Dignity, Theology and Disability*, Eds J. Claassns, L. Swartz and L. Hansen, pp. 43–54, Cape Town, Conference Rap.

Kuppers, P. 2014. Crip time, *Tikkun Magazine*, 29, 29–30.

Lane-Fox, M. 2010. Digital manifesto for a networked nation [Online]. Available at: http://raceonline2012.org/manifesto [Accessed 5 December 2018].

Lewis, C.S. 1940. *The Problem of Pain*, London, The Centenary Press.

Liddiard, K. 2013. Reflections on the process of researching disabled people's sexual lives, *Social Research Online*, 18, 10.

Liddiard, K. 2014a. The work of disabled identities in intimate relationships, *Disability and Society*, 29(1), 115–128.

Liddiard, K. 2014b. "I never felt like she was just doing it for the money": The intimate (gendered) realities of purchasing sexual pleasure and intimacy, *Sexualities*, 17(7), 837–855.

Liddiard, K. 2014c. Liking for like's sake: the commodification of disability on Facebook, *Journal of Developmental Disabilities*, 20(3), 94–101.

Liddiard, K. 2018a. *The Intimate Lives of Disabled People*, London, Routledge (ISBN 978-1-4094-6090-9).

Liddiard, K. 2018b. The Co-Researcher Collective [Online]. Available at: https://livinglifetothefullest.org/the-co-researcher-collective/ [Accessed 20 December 2021].

Liddiard, K., Runswick-Cole, K., Goodley, D., Whitney, S., Vogelmann, E. and Watts, L. 2018. "I was excited by the idea of a project that focuses on those unasked questions": Co-producing disability research with disabled young people, *Children and Society*, 33(2), 154–167.

Liddiard, K. and Slater, J. 2017. "Like, pissing yourself is not a particularly attractive quality, let's be honest": learning to contain through youth, adulthood, disability and sexuality, *Sexualities Special Issue: Disability and Sexual Corporeality*, 21(3), 319–333.

Liddiard, K., Runswick-Cole, K., Goodley, D., Spurr, R., Whitney, S., Vogelmann, E., Watts, L. and Evans, K. 2021. "Why would I go to hospital if it's not going to try and save me?": Disabled young people's experiences of the Covid crisis. In *Being Human in Covid-19*, Eds P. Martin, W. Pearce, S. De Saille and K. Liddiard, pp. 60–67, Bristol, Bristol University Press.

Littlechild, R., Tanner, D. and Hall, K. 2015. Co-research with older people: perspectives on impact, *Qualitative Social Work*, 14, 18–35.

Living Life to the Fullest Project Blog. 2017. #ARTSRETREAT2017 DAY ONE ... [Online]. Available at: https://livinglifetothefullest.org/2017/10/24/artsretreat2017-day-one/ [Accessed 4 November 2021].

Ljuslinder, K., Ellis, K. and Vikström, L. 2020. Cripping time – understanding the life course through the lens of ableism, *Scandinavian Journal of Disability Research*, 22(1), 35–38.

Lonsdale, S. 1990. *Women and Disability: The Experience of Disability Among Women*, Basingstoke, Macmillan.

Mahase, E. 2021. Covid-19: all adults on learning disability register should be prioritised for vaccination, says advisory committee, *British Medical Journal*, 372, 547.

Mallett, R. and Runswick-Cole, K. 2014. *Approaching Disability: Critical Issues and Perspectives*, Abingdon, Routledge.

Marx, K. 1843. *A Contribution to the Critique of Hegel's Philosophy of Right*, Paris., Cambridge University Press.

Mckinnon, A. 2017. Religion and Social Class: Theory and Method after Bourdieu, *Sociological Research Online*, 22(1), 1–13.

McRuer, R. 2006. *Crip Theory: Cultural Signs of Queerness and Disability*, New York, NY, New York University Press.

Michalko, R. 1999. *The Two in One: Walking with Smokie, Walking with Blindness*, Philadelphia, PA: Temple University Press.

Mingus, M. 2010a. Interdependency (excerpts from several talks) [Online]. Available at: https://leavingevidence.wordpress.com/2010/01/22/ interdependency-exerpts-from-several-talks/ [Accessed 4 November 2021].

Mingus, M. 2010b. Wherever you are is where I want to be: crip solidarity [Online]. Available at: https://leavingevidence.wordpress.com/2010/05/03/ where-ever-you-are-is-where-i-want-to-be-crip-solidarity/ [Accessed 30 November 2021].

Mingus, M. 2011. Access intimacy: the missing link [Online]. Available at: https://leavingevidence.wordpress.com/2011/05/05/access-intimacy-the-missing-link/ [Accessed 9 February 2022].

Mingus, M. 2017. Forced intimacy: an ableist norm [Online]. Available at: https://leavingevidence.wordpress.com/2017/08/06/forced-intimacy-an-ableist-norm/ [Accessed 30 November 2021].

Mitchell, W. 2010. 'I know how I feel': listening to young people with life-limiting conditions who have learning and communication impairments, *Qualitative Social Work*, 9, 185–203.

National Audit Office. 2011. Oversight of special education for young people aged 16–25 [Online]. Available at: https://www.nao.org.uk/wp-content/ uploads/2011/11/10121585.pdf [Accessed on 21 February 2019].

Nind, M. 2008. *Conducting qualitative research with people with learning, communication and other disabilities: methodological challenges*, ESRC National Centre for Research Methods Review Paper, National Centre for Research Methods.

Nind, M. 2014. *What Is Inclusive Research?*, London, Bloomsbury.

Nind, M., Wiles, R., Bengry-Howell, A. and Crow, G. 2012. Methodological innovation and research ethics: forces in tension or forces in harmony?. *Qualitative Research*, 13, 650–667.

Obst, P.L. and Stafurik, J. 2010. Online we are all able bodied: online psychological sense of community and social support found through membership of disability-specific websites promotes well-being for people living with a physical disability, *Journal of Community and Applied Social Psychology*, 20, 525–531.

Öhman, C. and Floridi, L. 2017. The political economy of death in the age of information: a critical approach to the digital afterlife industry, *Minds and Machines*, 27(4), 639–662.

Oliver, M. 1990. *The Politics of Disablement*, Oxford, Oxford University Press.

Oliver, M. 1992. Changing the social relations of research production, *Disability & Society*, 11, 115–120.

Oliver, M. 1996. *Understanding Disability: From Theory to Practice*, Basingstoke, The Macmillan Press.

Olsen, A. and Carter, C. 2016. Responding to the needs of people with learning disabilities who have been raped: co-production in action, *Tizard Learning Disability Review*, 21, 1–9.

Olsen, R. and Clarke, H. 2003. *Parenting and Disability: Disabled Parents' Experiences of Raising Children*, Bristol, Policy Press.

Ossei-Owusu, S. 2021. *Coronavirus and politics of disposability* [Online]. Available at: http://bostonreview.net/class-inequality-race-politics/shaun-ossei-owusu-coronavirus-and-politics-disposability [Accessed on 21 May 2021].

Overboe, J. 1999. Difference in itself: validating disabled people's lived experiences, *Body & Society*, 5(4), 17–29.

Pearson, C. and Trevisan, F. 2015. Disability activism in the new media ecology: campaigning strategies in the digital era, *Disability and Society*, 30, 924–940.

Plummer, K. 2003. *Intimate Citizenship: Private Decision and Public Dialogues*, London, University of Washington Press.

Pluquailec, J. 2018. Thinking and doing consent and advocacy in disabled children's childhood studies research. In *The Palgrave Handbook of Disabled Children's Childhood Studies*, Eds K. Runswick-Cole, T. Curran and K. Liddiard, pp. 213–229, Basingstoke, Palgrave Ltd.

Price-Robertson, R. and Duf, C. 2016. Realism, materialism and the assemblage: thinking psychologically with Manuel DeLanda, *Theory & Psychology*, 26(1), 58–76.

Rabiee, P., Sloper, P. and Beresford, B. 2005. Doing research with children and young people who do not use speech for communication, *Children & Society*, 19, 385–396.

Rabinow, P. and Rose, N. 2006. Biopower today, *BioSocieties*, 1, 195–217.

Ramilow, T.R. 2006. Bodies in the borderlands: Gloria Anzaldúa's and David Wojnarowicz's mobility machines, *Race, Ethnicity, Disability, and Literature*, 31(3), 169–187.

Rayner, J.A., Pyett, P. and Astbury, J. 2010. The medicalisation of 'tall' girls: a discourse analysis of medical literature on the use of synthetic oestrogen to reduce female height, *Social Science & Medicine*, 71(6), 1076–1083.

Reeve, D. 2002. Negotiating psycho-emotional dimensions of disability and their influence on identity constructions, *Disability & Society*, 17(5), 493–508.

Reeve, D. 2004. Psycho-emotional dimensions of disability and the social model. In *Implementing the Social Model of Disability: Theory and Research*, Eds C. Barnes and G. Mercer, pp. 83–100, Leeds, The Disability Press.

Reeve, D. 2012. Psycho-emotional disablism: the missing link?' In *Routledge Handbook of Disability Studies*, Eds N. Watson, A. Roulstone and C. Thomas, pp. 78–92, London, Routledge.

Reinders, H. 2012. "Doing theology and disability" in Europe, *Journal of Religion, Disability & Health*, 16(4), 439–442.

Reynolds, T.E. 2008. *Vulnerable Communion. A Theology of Disability and Hospitality*, Grand Rapids, MI, Brazos.

Reynolds, T.E. 2012. Theology and disability: changing the conversation. In *Searching for Dignity: Conversations on Human Dignity, Theology and Disability*, Eds J. Claassens, L. Swartz and L. Hansen, pp. 17–31, Cape Town, Conference Rap.

Rohr, R. 2016. God's most distressing disguise [Online]. Available at: https://cac.org/gods-most-distressing-disguise-2016-03-23/ [Accessed on 4 June 2020].

Rohr, R. 2019. In Christ [Online]. Available at: https://cac.org/in-christ-2019-02-27/ [Accessed on 21 May 2021].

Runswick-Cole, K. 2010. Living with dying and disablism: death and disabled children, *Disability and Society*, 7(1), 813–826.

Runswick-Cole, K. 2014. "Us" and "them"? The limits and possibilities of a politics of neurodiversity in neoliberal times, *Disability & Society*, 29(7), 1117–1129.

Runswick-Cole, K., Curran, T. and Liddiard, K. 2017. The everyday worlds of disabled children. In *Disability, Normalcy and the Everyday*, Eds G. Thomas and D. Sakellariou, pp. 41–61, Basingstoke, Palgrave Ltd.

Runswick-Cole, K., Curran, T. and Liddiard, K. Eds 2018. *The Palgrave Handbook of Disabled Children's Childhood Studies*, Basingstoke, Palgrave Ltd.

Runswick-Cole, K. and Goodley, D. 2017. 'The disability commons': re-thinking motherhood through disability. In *Palgrave Handbook of Disabled Children's Childhood Studies*, Eds K. Runswick-Cole, T. Curran and K. Liddiard, pp. 231–247, Basingstoke, Palgrave.

Ryan, S. 2017. *Justice for Laughing Boy: Connor Sparrowhawk – A Death by Indifference*, London, Jessica Kingsley Publishers.

Ryan, S. and Runswick-Cole, K. 2008. Repositioning mothers: mothers, disabled children and disability studies, *Disability & Society*, 23(3), 199–210.

Sakellariou, D. 2006. If not the disability, then what? Barriers to reclaiming sexuality following spinal cord injury, *Sexuality and Disability*, 24, 101–111.

Samuels, E. 2017. Six ways of looking at crip time, *Disability Studies Quarterly*, 37(3).

Saur, E. and Sidorkin, A.M. 2018. Disability, dialogue, and the posthuman, *Studies in Philosophy and Education*, 37, 567–578.

Save the Children. 2000. *Young People as Researchers: A Learning Resource Pack*, London, Save the Children.

Schutz, K. and Gyula, N. 2018. The controversy of religion and psychosis, *The Journal of Religion & Theology*, 2(2), 19–25.

Scott, D. 2000. The re-enchantment of humanism: an interview with Sylvia Wynter, *Small Axe*, 8, 119–207.

Seymour, J.E. 1999. Revisiting medicalisation and 'natural' death, *Social Science & Medicine*, 49(5), 691–704.

Seymour, W.S. 2001. In the flesh or online? Exploring qualitative research methodologies, *Qualitative Research*, 1, 147–168.

Shakespeare, T. 2006. *Disability Rights and Wrongs*, Oxon, Routledge.

Shakespeare, T., Gillespie-Sells, K. and Davies, D. 1996. *Untold Desires: The Sexual Politics of Disability*, London, Cassell.

Shakespeare, T., Ndagire, F. and Seketi, Q.E. 2021. Triple jeopardy: disabled people and the COVID-19 pandemic, *The Lancet*, 397(10282), 1331–1333.

Shildrick, M. 2009. *Dangerous Discourse of Disability, Subjectivity and Sexuality*, New York, NY, Palgrave Macmillan.

Shyman, E. 2016. The reinforcement of ableism: normality, the medical model of disability, and humanism in applied behavior analysis and ASD, *Intellectual and Developmental Disabilities*, 54(5), 366–376.

Slater, J. and Liddiard, K. 2018. Why disability studies scholars must challenge transmisogyny and transphobia, *Canadian Journal of Disability Studies*, 7(2), 83–93.

Spurr, R. 2019. Questions worth asking: speen festival [Online]. Available at: https://livinglifetothefullesttoolkitcom.files.wordpress.com/2019/12/ruth-questions-worth-asking-speen-festival-2019.pdf [Accessed 20 May 2021].

St. Pierre, J. 2015. Cripping communication: speech, disability, and exclusion in liberal humanist and posthumanist discourse, *Communication Theory*, 25(3), 330–348.

Strnadová, I., Cumming, T.M., Knox, M., Parmenter, T. and Welcome to Our Class Research Group. 2014. Building an inclusive research team: the importance of team building and skills training, *Journal of Applied Research in Intellectual Disabilities*, 27(1), 13–22.

Strnadová, I., Walmsley, J., Johnson, K. and Cumming, T.M. 2015. Diverse faces of inclusive research: reflecting on three research studies, *Scandinavian Journal of Disability Research*, 18, 52–64.

Staden, H. 1998. Alertness to the needs of others: a study of the emotional labour of caring, *Journal of Advanced Nursing*, 27(1), 147–156.

Swain, J., Heyman, B. and Gillman, M. 1998. Public research, private concerns: ethical issues in the use of open-ended interviews with people who have learning difficulties, *Disability & Society*, 13, 21–36.

Swartz, L. 2013. Between faith and doubt: training members of disabled people's organisations in Southern Africa in basic research skills. In *Searching for Dignity: Conversations on Human Dignity, Theology and Disability*, Eds J. Claassens, L. Swartz and L. Hansen, pp. 81–90, Cape Town, Conference Rap.

Taleporos, G. and McCabe, M. 2001. The impact of physical disability on body esteem, *Sexuality and Disability*, 19, 293–308.

Taylor, S. 2017. *Beasts of Burden: Animal and Disability Liberation*, New York, NY, The New Press.

Thomas, C. 1999. *Female Forms: Experiencing and Understanding Disability*, Buckingham, Open University Press.

Thomas, C. 2007. *Sociologies of Disability and Illness: Contested Ideas in Disability Studies and Medical Sociology*, Basingstoke, Palgrave Macmillan.

Thompson, S.A., Bryson, M. and De Castell, S. 2001. Prospects for identity formation for lesbian, gay, or bisexual persons with developmental disabilities, *International Journal of Disability, Development and Education*, 48(1), 53–65.

Titchkosky, T. and Michalko, R. 2009. *Rethinking Normalcy: A Disability Studies Reader*, Toronto, Canadian Scholars' Press.

Tuffrey-Wijne, I., Bernal, J. and Hollins, S. 2008. Doing research on people with learning disabilities, cancer and dying: ethics, possibilities and pitfalls, *British Journal of Learning Disabilities*, 36, 185–190.

United Nations. 1989. *Convention on the Rights of the Child*, London, HMSO.

Vehmas, S. and Watson, N. 2014. Moral wrongs, disadvantages, and disability: a critique of critical disability studies, *Disability and Society*, 29(4), 638–650.

Walmsley, J. 2004. Inclusive learning disability research: the (nondisabled) researcher's role, *British Journal of Learning Disabilities*, 32, 65–71.

Watling, S. 2011. Digital exclusion: coming out from behind closed doors, *Disability and Society*, 26, 491–495.

Watts, L. 2017. My social media will – Lucy Watts MBE [Online]. Available at: https://digitallegacyassociation.org/lucy-watts-social-media-will/ [Accessed 12 December 2021].

Watts, L. 2018. *Social media and digital legacy* [Online]. Available at: https://livinglifetothefullest.org/2018/06/22/social-media-and-digital-legacy/ [Accessed 12 December 2021].

Waxman-Fiduccia, B. 2000. Current issues in sexuality and the disability movement, *Sexuality and Disability*, 18(3), 167–174.

Wendell, S. 1996. *The Rejected Body: Feminist Philosophical Reflections on Disability*, London, Routledge & Kegan Paul.

Whitney, S. 2018. Death and dying: It's biography not biology that matters most at the end [Online]. Available at: https://livinglifetothefullest.

org/2019/02/04/death-and-dying-its-biography-not-biology-that-matters-most-at-the-end/ [Accessed 23 December 2021].

Whitney, S., Bakalov, N., Liddiard, K., Frediani, A., Runswick-Cole, K., Goodley, D. and Evans, K. 2020. *The Canine Care Project: A report into disabled young people's experiences of their assistance dogs*, University of Sheffield and Canine Partners.

Whitney, S., Liddiard, K., Goodley, D., Runswick-Cole, K., Vogelmann, E., Evans, K., Watts (MBE), L. and Aimes, C. 2019. Working the edges of posthuman disability studies: theorising with young disabled people with life-limiting impairments, *Sociology of Health and Illness*, 41(8), 1473–1487.

Why can't we dream? A co-production toolkit: University of Sheffield [Online]. Available at: https://whycantwedream.co.uk/ [Accessed 13 December 2021]

Wilkerson, A. 2002. Disability, sex radicalism and political agency, *NSWA Journal*, 14(3), 33–57.

Williams, S. (n.d.). Weakness, Baker's dictionary of theology, n.p. [Online]. Available at: https://www.biblestudytools.com/dictionaries/bakers-evangelical-dictionary/weakness.html [Accessed 4 June 2020].

Wood, J.D. and Milo, E. 2001. Fathers' grief when a disabled child dies, *Death Studies*, 8, 635–661.

Yu, H., Goggin, G., Fisher, K. and Li, B. 2019. Introduction: disability participation in the digital economy, *Information, Communication & Society*, 22(4), 467–473.

Zarb, G. 1992. On the road to Damascus: first steps towards changing the relations of disability research production, *Disability, Handicap & Society*, 7, 125–138.

Zola, I.K. 1998. The language of disability politics and practice, *Australian Disability Review* [Online]. Available at: http:www.disabilitymuseum.corg/lib/docs/813.card.htm [Accessed 14 May 2018].

INDEX

Ableism, 3, 126
   legacies, 144
Absence of ability, 15
'Access intimacy', 7
Accessibility, 29, 35, 98
Activism, 11, 12, 34, 39, 143
Activist legacies, 142–143
Advocate, 60, 105
'Agents of psychoemotional
   disablism', 95
Analysis Workshop, 120
Animal–human relationships,
   44–45
Arts-informed approaches, 32
Assessment, 123
Assistance dog
   Ethan, co-researcher Sally and,
      49–53, 56–58
   experiences of disabled young
      people, 44
   Folly, co-researcher Katy and,
      53–55
   importance in disabled young
      people, 46–47
   Living Life to the Fullest
      Project, 44
Assistance dogs, 48
Autobiographical legacies,
   143–144

Barriers
   disabled young people, 86–87
   disabled young people
      identifying, 127
   experience, 7
   external, 17, 107, 127

internalized, 17
   material, 13
   physical, 83
   psycho-emotional, 17
   in social world, 26
   societal, 16
   structural, 62
Big Question approach, 117–118
Body
   disabled, 91
   image, 82–83
   life beyond, 21
   material, 80

Canine Care Project, 9, 44, 48
Care, 56–58, 90–93
Career, 5, 137
Caring, 56–58
Childhood, 14, 26
   sociology of, 27
   Western, 128
Children in research, 26–28
Co-production, 16, 26, 122
Co-production Toolkit, 8, 117,
   119, 122–123
Co-Researcher Collective, 5–8, 11,
   26, 115, 126, 129
   contesting power imbalances,
      31–32
Collaborative analysis, 34–36
Connection, 75–77
   posthuman, 43–60
Covid-19 pandemic, 38, 47, 67
Crip
   accessible cultures, 114
   accessible spaces, 111

accessible systems, 112–114
accessible technology, 112
accessible times, 111–112
alternative workplaces, 114
crip-solidarity legacies, 144
time, 26, 40, 101
Cripspiration, 86
Critical disability studies, 12–17,
    26, 100
children and young people in
    research, 26–28
Co-Researcher Collective,
    31–32
collaborative analysis, 34–36
disability research, 37–41
disabled young people, 28–30
embodied knowledge, 36–37
virtual spaces, 37–41
young people, 37–41
Critical posthumanities, 20–22
Cultures accessible in workplace,
    114

Data
analysing, 36
artistic, 35
collection, 117
from disabled young people,
    48–49
gathering, 38
narrative, 35
Dating, 80
online, 80, 86–90
Death, 125
illness, threat and progression,
    131–133
leaving legacies, 139–144
life and, 127–129
life and living with, 129
life expectancies, 133–137
living with grief, 137–139
surviving and thriving, 129–131
Department for Work and
    Pensions (DWP), 113
Desires, 2, 14, 81

Digital legacies, 140–141
Digital lives, 85–90
Disability, 11, 82, 101
critical disability studies, 12–17
critical posthumanities, 20–22
disabled young people, 61
DisHuman perspective, 12,
    22–23
and faith, 61
faith at centre, 64
hope and suffering, 65–67
humanism, 17–19
interdependency and
    vulnerability, 67–70
love, 'otherness' and
    marginalized, 70–71
in online dating, 86–90
research, 37–41
Sally's journey with illness,
    disability and faith, 64–65
self-worth and identity through
    faith, 72–74
studies, 62–64
Disabled
parenting, 97
people, 55, 67, 79
young people, 28–30, 140–144
young person, 48
Disabled Children's Childhood
    Studies, 4, 14, 26, 124
Disabled feminists, 97, 127
Disablism, 126
Disclosure in online dating, 86–90
Discrimination, 109
DisHuman approach, 44
DisHuman perspective, 12,
    22–23
Distress protocol, 128
Dogs, assistance, 49–58
Dying, 35, 72, 126, 138

Economic and Social Research
    Council (ESRC), 116
Emancipatory disability research,
    25, 27

Emotional labour, 100–102
  and advocacy, 105–108
  and body work, 102–103
  cripping workplace, 108–114
  in medicalised spaces, 103–104
  social care, 105–108
Emotional support, 51–52
Emotional wellbeing, 53–55
Employment, 64, 113
Employment and support
  allowance (ESA), 113
Equality Act, 110
ESRC Festival of Social Science,
  121
Ethics, 119, 120
Exclusion, 3, 20, 62

Faith
Faith, disability and, 61–74
Feminists, 15, 20, 97, 127
Future, 127–137

Greenacre School, 116
Grief, 137–139
Grounding, 54–55

Happiness, 137
Health, 29, 56
'Higher order thinking skills', 123
Hope, 65–67
Hospitalisation, 40
Human
  animal–human relationships,
    43–60
  diversity, 18
  human–animal interrelations, 21
  life, 12, 21
  life beyond human species, 21
  predicaments, 20
  productivity, 16
  right, 12, 19
  value, 101, 110
  value of disability, 1
Humanism, 12, 17–19, 45
Humanist concept, 46

Identity, 35–36, 38, 44, 49–53
Illness, 131–133
Impairment, 13, 30, 85
  in digital intimacies, 80
  internal experience of, 127
  life-threatening impairment, 98
  negative impacts of, 40
  progression, 92, 95, 132, 134
Inclusion, 28, 29
Independence, 50–51
'Inspiration porn', 86
Institute for the Study of Human
  (iHuman), 37
Interdependencies, 46–49
Interdependency, 67–70
Internet, 38
Intersectionality, 23
Interspecies relationships, 51–52
Intimacy, 35, 39, 85
  disability and, 84–85
  for disabled young people, 80,
    98
  forced, 108
  posthuman, 51
  rights and access to, 81
  sexuality and, 94
  trans-species, 57
Intimate legacies, 140

Joy, 34, 130
Justice, 38

Labour, 99 (see also Emotional
  labour)
Lasting power of attorney (LPA),
  141
Learning, 123
Legacy, 2, 8, 127, 131
  crip-solidarity legacies, 144
  digital, 142
  for disabled young people,
    140–144
  leaving, 139
  physical, 144
'Lethal binaries', 67

LGBT+ disabled young person, 93
Liberal humanism, 18
Life expectancies, 127, 133–137
Life limiting and life-threatening
    impairments (LL/LTIs), 2,
    13, 94, 99, 125
Life-threatening condition, 49, 80,
    96, 137
Living Life to the Fullest Project,
    1, 2, 11–12, 26, 29, 31–32,
    34–35, 37, 39–40, 43–45,
    47, 51, 56, 111, 140
  Canine Care Project, 9
  Co-Researcher Collective, 5–8
  collaborative analysis, 8
  context of LL/LTIs, 3
  crip alternatives, 100
  disabled children's childhood
    studies, 4
  explored lives of disabled
    young people living with
    LL/LTIs, 127
  focus on meaning of ethics, 119
  legacy from, 122, 144
  impact of living with
    knowledge, 73
  voices of disabled young people
    in, 59–60
Loneliness Project, 116
Love, 17, 70–71, 90–93

Marginalisation, 3, 41, 45, 64, 69,
    70–71, 106
'Me Before You' (film), 84–85
'Medical model perspective', 17
Medicalisation, 18
Mental health, 53–55
Methodology
  co-production, 5
  rethinking, 32–34
  revolutionary, 9
'Missing People's Humanities', 20

National Audit Office, 110
Non-disabled people, 107

Non-governmental organisations
    (NGOs), 4
Normalisation, 137

Online dating
  disability in, 86–90
  disclosure in, 86–90
'Otherness', 70–71
Oppression, 38, 62, 63

Parents, 4, 5, 30, 34, 110
Participants, 3, 6, 32, 35, 37, 40, 82
'Permitted work' scheme, 113
Personal assistants (PAs), 55
Personal independence payment
    (PIP), 113
Physical wellbeing, 57–58
Posthuman connections
  Canine Care Project, 44
  Co-researcher Katy and
    assistance dog Folly, 53–55
  Co-researcher Sally and
    assistance dog Ethan,
    49–53, 56–58
  connections with assistance
    animals, 45–46
  interdependencies, 46–49
  motivation, confidence and
    challenges, 58–60
  posthuman disability studies, 43
Power, 68
  contesting power imbalances,
    31–32
  of gaze, 38
  of God's love, 70
  of others' Ableist perceptions,
    81–83
Privacy, 39, 90, 93
Professionals, 30, 104, 106
Progression, 131–133
Pruning process, 72
Purple Patch Arts, 32

Real life (RL), 38
Reciprocity, 55

Relationships, 5, 35, 48, 94, 116
Religion, 61, 62–64, 75
Remote, 111
Reproductive futures, 94–98
Resus and Intensive Care, 56
Rethinking method, 32–34
Rights, 19, 27, 80
Romantic relationship, 96, 135–136

Schools, 115
  co-production toolkit, 122
  ESRC Festival of Social Science,
    121
  Greenacre School, 116
  learning and assessment, 123
  SEND Teacher, 118
  working in, 117–120
  working in and with university,
    120–121
Seldom, 29
Self-esteem, 17, 34, 59, 80
Self-worth and identity through
    faith, 72–74
Sex, 80, 90–93
Sexuality, 79
  digital lives, 85–90
  feeling, 83–85
  intimate and reproductive
    futures, 94–98
  intimate selves, 85–90
  loneliness, difficulties in
    socialising, 83–85
  mediating love, sex and care,
    90–93
  power of others' Ableist
    perceptions, 81–83
Social care, 105–108
Social inclusion, 52–53
Social media, 85–86
Social model, 108
Solidarity, 7, 8
Space, 101
  accessible in workplaces, 111
Special educational need and
    disability (SEND), 116

Suffering, 65–67
Support, emotional, 51–53
Surviving, 129–131
Systems accessible in workplaces,
    112–114

Technology accessible in
    workplaces, 112
Temporalities
  of 'work', 46
  of qualitative methods, 40
  of research, 26, 40–41
Theory, 12, 44
Thriving, 129–131
Times accessible in workplaces,
    111–112
Toolkit, co-production, 8, 117,
    119, 122–123

United Nations Convention on
    Rights of Persons with
    Disabilities, 19
'Unobtrusive observation
    approaches', 38
Utopian scenario, 16

Virtual spaces, 37–41
Virtual technologies, 38
Vulnerability, 57, 67–70, 75, 87,
    126–127

What Matters? project, 116–117,
    123
Why Can't We Dream?, 8, 117,
    119, 122
Work, 9, 90, 99–100
  advocacy, 105, 106
  conventional world of, 107
  disabled people, 104, 109, 114
  emotional, 126, 132
  emotional labour and body
    work, 102–103
  face-to-face, 7
  forms of, 36
  from home, 110

level of, 104
paid, 100–101, 108–109
permitted, 113
temporalities of, 40
Workplace
    accessible cultures, 114
    accessible spaces, 111
    accessible systems, 112–114
    accessible technology, 112
    accessible times, 111–112
    crip alternatives, 109–111
    cripping, 108
    social model, 108

Young people
    and assistance dogs, 45
    capacity of, 27
    care and support for disabled,
        60
    democratisation of researching
        with, 27
    disability and disclosure in
        online dating, 86–90

disabled, 4–9, 34–35, 46–47,
    58–59
    expectation role, 94–98
    faith and, 73
    formation of identity, 81
    living with LL/LTIs, 2–3,
        12–13, 17, 30, 33–35
    mediating love, sex and care in
        disabled, 90–93
    in research, 26–28
    social media and, 85–86
    studies of, 14
    in The Living Life to the Fullest
        Project, 59
    used interview space, 80
    virtual spaces, disability
        research and, 37–41, 80
    Young People as Researchers,
        28–29
Youth
    disability studies in, 14, 128
    and friendship, 137
    social media and, 86